Spiritual
Warfare

Spiritual Warfare

Winning the Daily Battle with Satan

RAY C. STEDMAN

MULTNOMAH

Portland, Oregon 97266

Unless otherwise identified, all Scripture references are from the Revised Standard Version of the Bible, copyright 1946, 1952, © 1971, 1973, Division of Christian Education, National Council of the Churches of Christ in the USA. Used by permission.

Cover design by Phil Malyon and Judy Quinn
Photograph by Peter Grant

SPIRITUAL WARFARE
© 1975 by Ray C. Stedman
Published by Multnomah Press
Portland, Oregon 97266

Published in cooperation with Discovery Foundation,
Palo Alto, California

Printed in the United States of America

Library of Congress Cataloging in Publication Data

Stedman, Ray C.
    Spiritual warfare.

    Reprint. Originally published: Waco, Tex. : Word Books, 1975.
    1. Christian life—1960-   2. Devil.   I. Title.
BV4501.2.S739   1985   248.4   85-2893
ISBN 0-88070-094-7 (pbk.)

              89 90 91 – 10 9 8 7 6 5 4

CONTENTS

PREFACE

Behind the confusion and uncertainty that exists today on every hand lies the craft and power of the great spiritual being which Jesus called "the ruler of this world," the devil. Despite the recent surge of interest in the occult and satanism, there is still a woeful ignorance on the part of Christians everywhere as to how to deal with the devil and his wiles.

Much is being written today about dealing with demonic influence and possession, but the Christian world seems to know little or nothing about how to recognize the indirect control of believers through what the Bible calls "the flesh" and even less about what to do with it.

It is the purpose of this book to give help where it is most needed: in the day-to-day conflict where the devil's craft reaches us in terms of hostilities, worries, resentments, fears, disappointments, and nameless depressions of spirit. Here is where the great resources of Christ are more needed than at any other time.

I gladly acknowledge my great debt to the fine series of studies of Dr. Martyn Lloyd-Jones on Ephesians 6, published serially in *The Westminister Record,* and to the pastoral staff of Peninsula Bible Church for their unfailing encouragement.

In a very real sense, those of us who believe in the Lord Jesus Christ are engaged in a battle. But the forces we face are not clothed in flesh; they are not human agencies. Rather they are the deadly pantheon of spiritual hosts of wickedness, invisible and dedicated to our destruction.

These forces are under the authority of the one who is the father of lies, the prince of darkness, the devil himself. Only by recognizing him as real, as the Scriptures clearly declare, can we begin to understand the meaning of life as it really is. Only then can we comprehend the vital necessity of putting on the whole armor of God which far from being merely a figure of speech is in fact Christ himself, as he is to us.

In our helplessness, once fully realized, we have been given three specific steps to take which will enable us to be conquerors. First, we are to appropriate by thoughtful consideration the complete protection of Christ. Then, fully armed, we are to pray. Prayer must be the result of our acceptance of the armor of God, the action which fulfills the thought.

Finally, in the face of whatever attacks God allows Satan to mount against us, we are to stand firm in our faith with the certain knowledge that the battle is the Lord's. Our faith in his victory, already accomplished, is what overcomes the world.

Ray C. Stedman

Finally, be strong in the Lord and in the strength of his might. Put on the whole armor of God, that you may be able to stand against the wiles of the devil. For we are not contending against flesh and blood, but against the principalities, against the powers, against the world rulers of this present darkness, against the spiritual hosts of wickedness in the heavenly places. Therefore take the whole armor of God, that you may be able to withstand in the evil day, and having done all, to stand (Ephesians 6:10-13).

1
THE FORCES
WE FACE

God is not interested in religion, but he is tremendously interested in life. You cannot read the New Testament without realizing that the Lord Jesus did not care a whit for the Sabbath regulations of his day when they were set against the need of a broken man for healing. God is not interested in stained-glass windows, organ solos, congregational hymns, or even pastoral prayers half so much as he is in producing love-filled homes, generous hearts, and brave men and women who can live right in the midst of the world and keep their heads and hearts undefiled.

I am deeply convinced that we can only understand life when we see it as the Bible sees it. That is why the

Word of God was given. In the world of organized human society with its commerce, trade, recreation, and all the familiar makeup of life, we are continually exposed to illusions which are mingled indistinguishably with reality. We are confronted with distorted perspectives, twisted motives, uncertain hopes, and untested programs.

But when we come to the Bible we learn the truth. Here reality is set before us—the world as it really is. When we get down to the bare essentials of life and strip off all the confusing illusion, we find it is exactly what the Bible records it to be. Here is where our perspectives are set straight, here is where we get our value systems righted and our dreams weighed and evaluated as to whether they are real or only make-believe.

We may not like what we read in the Bible from time to time, but we shall only succeed in deceiving ourselves if we reject it. It is up to us to listen to the words of Jesus and his apostles, for they are the authority which corrects us; we are not the authority that corrects them. Let us stop this silly business of trying to sit in judgment upon the insights of the Lord Jesus Christ. We Christians must continually reduce every argument we hear today to this simple consideration: "Am I to accept this person's word or the word of Christ? If this agrees with what he says, fine; it is truth. But if it does not, then I must decide whether the challenging authority is greater or less than Jesus Christ." As Christians, we are continually confronted with choices as to whether we will accept the puny, flimsy, uncertain authority of a mere man or the certain, solid, and clear word of the Lord Jesus Christ.

Life Is Not a Bowl of Cherries!

In this important passage near the end of Ephesians the apostle Paul sets forth his analysis of life, especially as it relates to a Christian. To begin with, we will look at the passage only from an introductory viewpoint to see what Paul brings out about the nature of life in general, and then we will take a closer look at the specific character which he says a Christian life assumes. This section begins:

> *Finally, be strong in the Lord and in the strength of his might. Put on the whole armor of God, that you may be able to stand against the wiles of the devil. For we are not contending against flesh and blood, but against the principalities, against the powers, against the world rulers of this present darkness, against the spiritual hosts of wickedness in the heavenly places. Therefore take the whole armor of God, that you may be able to withstand in the evil day, and having done all, to stand (Ephesians 6:10-13).*

It is very clear in this passage that Paul's view of the basic characteristic of life can be put in one word: *struggle.* Life, he says, is a conflict, a combat, a continual wrestling. This is, of course, confirmed constantly by our experience. We should all like to think of ourselves as living in an idealistic world where everything goes right and we can spend our days in relaxation and enjoyment, with just enough work to keep us interested. This view is frequently embodied in some of the songs we sing.

> *We'll build a sweet little nest,*
> *Somewhere in the West,*
> *And let the rest of the world go by.*

Now, it is not wrong for us to dream those dreams. These romantic ideals are a kind of racial memory, the vestigial remains of what was once God's intent for human life, and in God's good order and time will again be possible to humans. But the apostle Paul is not dealing with that kind of life. He is coming to grips with life as it really is now, and he says life is a struggle, a conflict, a battle against opposing forces. If we attempt to draw aside, to get away from the struggle, we continually find ourselves being jarred back into reality. Some unpleasant fact intrudes itself into our beautiful world and refuses to go away.

We all know how this is. We must get back to work, our vacation is ended . . . the death of a loved one shocks us with all its ghastly emptiness and loneliness . . . we remember some pressing decision we must make, some threat to our prosperity or health, some disappointment in another person. We are constantly drawn back out of our dreams of ease and enjoyment to face the rough, hard realities of life.

Paul also says that this is a fluctuating struggle. We must learn to stand, he says, "in the evil day," implying that all days are not evil; some times will be worse than others. There are seasons in the passing of life when pressures are more intense, when problems are more insoluble, when everything seems to come upon us at once. These are what we recognize as evil days. Sometimes it is an actual day, sometimes it is a week, sometimes months. But thank God all of life is not that way. We are not *always* under pressure, we are not always being confronted with overpowering circumstances which call for agonizing decisions.

The reason we are not always under pressure is the grace of God. All of life would be an evil day, and much worse, were it not for the grace of God which continually operates to restrain the powers that are against us and to allow times of refreshment, recreation, enjoyment, and blessing. The truly tragic thing about human life is that we can take these times of refreshment, blessing, and glory and enjoy them without a single thought for the goodness of God which underlies them and makes them possible for us, and without a word of thanksgiving to God for them. This is the note on which Paul opens the Epistle to the Romans: "Do you presume upon the riches of his kindness and forbearance and patience? Do you not know that God's kindness is meant to lead you to repentance?" (Romans 2:4).

The Battle Defined

But here Paul says that these days, though not always the same in pressure, nevertheless constitute the general makeup of life. Life is an unending struggle, varying in intensity from time to time, but extending from the cradle to the grave. But he goes on now to analyze and define for us the nature of this struggle. We come now to that which is most important. For he says that the conflict is not against flesh and blood; that is, it is not a human problem, not a struggle of man against man. It may be a struggle *within* man, but it is not *between* men.

What would you answer if you were asked, "What is the thing that gives you the most difficulty in life; of what does the struggle of life consist?" Many would say that it is other human beings. There are the Communists, for instance, who are always causing difficulty. They can never let anything rest in this world but are forever stirring up some kind of trouble somewhere. And then there are the Republicans, or if you are on the other side, the Democrats. They never let anything rest either but are always making difficulties. In their bullheaded obstinacy they are continually refusing to see the light.

And let us not forget the Internal Revenue Service. Certainly they are devils, if there ever were any. And the county tax department! And don't leave out your wife—and her family! Or your husband and his family. Then how about our ancestors? . . . our heredity is at fault. It is because we are Scotch or Irish or Italian—our family has always been this way; we have always had hot tempers. And so it goes.

But the apostle says that you cannot explain life adequately on that level. You must look further and deeper than that. The battle is not against flesh and blood. Rather, it is against the whole human race that certain principalities and powers, world rulers of darkness, wicked spirits in high places are set. There is your problem, Paul says. Those are the enemies we are up against. And it is not just Christians who are opposed by these, but every man, everywhere. The whole race is opposed by the principalities and powers, the world rulers of this present darkness. There is Paul's positive explanation of the struggle of life.

I hasten to say that this declaration will only be fully believed and understood by Christians. The world either distorts this to the point of ridiculousness or it rejects it as unacceptable to the intelligent mind. Superstition has taken this great revelation and distorted it, twisted it, reduced it to a ridiculous pantheon of goblins, witches, spooks, and ghouls.

I am very well aware of the disdain, even contempt, with which the biblical concept of the devil and his cohorts, this kingdom of darkness, these principalities and powers and wicked spirits in high places, is received in many circles. There are those who say, "Are you going to insult our intelligence by talking about a personal devil? Surely you are not going back to those medieval concepts and tell us that the devil is the root of all our problems?"

I once spent an evening in Berlin discussing this whole problem with four or five intelligent churchmen—men who knew the Bible intimately. Though we never once opened a Bible, we spent the whole evening together discussing various passages, and I never referred to a single passage that they were not aware of and could not quote almost verbatim. Yet all of them rejected the idea of a devil. They could not believe in a personal devil. At the end of the evening they admitted that in their rejection of the devil, they also had no answers to the conundrums which life was continually presenting. We had to leave it there.

I am reminded of the story Billy Graham tells in response to this idea that there is no devil. A certain boxer was being badly beaten in a match. Battered and bruised, he leaned over the ropes and said to his trainer, "Please throw in the towel! This guy is killing me!" The trainer responded, "Oh no he's not. He's not even hitting you. He hasn't laid a glove on you!" And the boxer replied, "Well then, I wish you'd watch that referee—somebody is sure hitting me!" In similar fashion, the questions we must ask when challenged with this idea that there is no devil are, How do you explain what is going on in the world? How do you explain the entrenched evil in human affairs?

The Desperate Disease

Is it not clear that we cannot understand life, we cannot understand history, if we reject this proposition which the apostle brings out that behind the problems of the world, behind the evil which manifests itself in mankind, there is a hierarchy of evil spirits—the devil and his angels? There is an organized kingdom of principalities and powers at various levels of authority who sit as world rulers of the present darkness, wicked spirits in high places. The world says to the Christian, "Why talk about this kind of thing? Why don't you talk about something relevant? Why don't you Christians get busy and do something that will be meaningful today?"

But what could be more relevant than this teaching which puts its finger on the basic problem? What good is it to keep rushing around curing fevers but never stopping to analyze the disease? This is what is going on in our day. There is a serious disease at work in the human race, and it is constantly breaking out in little fevers. But if we content ourselves as physicians with giving aspirin for the fever and never once inquiring what the disease is, we have wasted our time. Talk about relevancy! This is what is relevant— to listen to this analysis of what is wrong with the world, what its disease is, and what the cure is. That is what this passage so vividly and so accurately sets before us.

This crippling disease is growing so desperate that even worldlings, non-Christians, are recognizing the inadequacy of their diagnosis. Listen to Carl Jung, the great Swiss psychologist and psychiatrist:

> *We stand perplexed and stupefied before the phenomena of Marxism and Bolshevism because* we know nothing about man *or, at any rate, have only a lopsided and distorted picture of him. If we had self-knowledge, that would not be the case. We stand face to face with the terrible question of evil and do not even know what is before us, let alone know what to pit against it. And even if we did know, we still could not understand how it could happen here.*

What a tremendously honest revelation of the ignorance of men in the face of life as it really is! Listen to this bewildered cry from U Thant, when he was Secretary General of the United Nations. Speaking before some sixty-seven distinguished scholars and statesmen from nineteen countries of the world, convened before an audience of 2500 people to talk about the requirements for world peace, this is the question he asked:

> *What element is lacking so that with all our skill and all our knowledge we still find ourselves in the dark valley of discord and enmity? What is it that inhibits us from going forward together to enjoy the fruits of human endeavor and to reap the harvest of human experience? Why is it that, for all our professed ideals, our hopes, and our skills, peace on earth is still a distant objective seen only dimly through the storms and turmoils of our present difficulties?*

As the world's great leaders face the dilemma of modern life, all they can say is, "What is wrong? What is the unknown element behind this? We cannot understand this, we do not know what is going on, we cannot grasp these things. What is it that is missing?"

No Isolated Claim

The apostle Paul has given the answer to the baffled, bewildered cry for light from a modern statesman's heart. Talk about a relevant Scripture! The world, Paul says, is in the grip of what he calls "world rulers of present darkness." (What an amazing phrase that is! We will look at it more closely in a later chapter.)

These world rulers of present darkness are headed by the devil, whom Scripture says is a fallen angel of malevolent power and cunning cleverness, against whom Christians are called to wrestle daily. Now, that is not the claim of an isolated passage of the Bible. That is the teaching of the Bible from beginning to end, from Genesis to Revelation, and especially *in* Genesis and Revelation.

The Lord Jesus himself put his finger on the whole problem when he said to certain men of his day, "You are of your father the devil, and your will is to do your father's desires. He was a murderer from the beginning, and has nothing to do with the truth, because there is no truth in him. When he lies, he speaks according to his own nature, for he is a liar and the father of lies" (John 8:44).

In that most amazing analysis the Lord stripped the devil of his disguises and revealed his true character—a liar and a murderer. What the devil does is related to what he is, just as what we do is precisely the result of what we are. Because the devil is a liar and a murderer, his work is to deceive and to destroy. There you have the explanation for all that has been going on in human history throughout the whole course of the record of man.

The devil has the ear of mankind. Scripture calls him "the god of this world." The world listens to him and to everything he says. But the devil does not tell the world the truth, but a lie, a very clever, a very beautiful, a very attractive lie which makes the world drool with desire. But the end of this lie is destruction, murder, death!—death in all its forms, not only ultimately the cessation of life but also death in its incipient forms of restlessness, boredom, frustration, meaninglessness, and emptiness. Whom the devil cannot deceive, he tries to destroy, and whom he cannot destroy, he attempts to deceive. There is the working of the devil.

The Call to Arms

"Well," you say, "this is all very depressing. I would rather not think about it." So would I, but I have discovered that you cannot get away from it that way. There is only one way in which we can ever handle this struggle and that is to be strong in the Lord and in the power of his might. That is the way of escape, and there is no other.

This is a call to intelligent combat. It is a call to us to be men, to fight the good fight, to stand fast in the faith, to be strong in the Lord right in the midst of the battle, in the midst of the world. You can hear the bugle in this, can you not? You can hear the trumpet call!

We must learn to recognize how these dark systems of the devil work, but more than that, we must learn the processes of overcoming them—not by flesh and blood, not by joining committees or mustering some kind of physical struggle against these forces. Paul says the weapons of our warfare are not carnal, not fleshly, they are not of the body. Our weapons are mighty, through God, unto the pulling down of strongholds and the bringing into captivity of every thought (Ah! there is the arena. It is the realm of ideas) . . . bringing into captivity every thought to the obedience of Christ. That is victory!

Do you think that is not challenging? That is the greatest challenge any ear can every hear! Do you think that is not demanding? That demands more courage and manhood than any other cause which has ever been known in the world! Do you think that is not exciting? That is the most exciting call which has ever gone out to men anywhere! "Be strong in the Lord and in the strength of his might!"

Our gracious Father, thank you for a truth that shatters us, startles us, wakens us, prods us, disturbs us. Thank you, Lord, for a word of reality which speaks to us in the midst of our complacency and lethargy and stirs us up to see life as it really is. How easily we would drift on in futile weakness, never raising a finger against the deterioration of life and the destruction of body and soul, were it not for this word of challenge which calls us back, wakes us up, and makes us to see. Lord, teach us to bow in humility before this word and to say to the Holy Spirit, "O great teacher of God, open these Scriptures, teach them to us, make them real." In Christ's name, amen.

When a strong man, fully armed, guards his own palace, his goods are in peace; but when one stronger than he assails him and overcomes him, he takes away his armor in which he trusted, and divides his spoil. He who is not with me is against me, and he who does not gather with me scatters (Luke 11:21-23).

2
BEGINNING
THE BATTLE

We have a challenge before us, clearly sounded in the passage from Ephesians which forms the basis for our study. In order to meet the challenge to be "strong in the Lord," we must expect to learn much about this kingdom of evil, these wicked spirits in high places who Paul says lie behind the insoluble problem of human evil.

The apostle indicates that the only ones who can successfully battle against the devil's forces are Christians. "For we are not contending against flesh and blood . . ." Who are the *we*? Surely this is not man in general, but these are Christians.

The world suffers because of the powers of evil, but

the Christian wrestles against them. Now, this is not a position that is peculiar to Paul, but it is a consistent teaching all through the Bible. The Bible indicates that all men are victims of these invisible forces. All men everywhere, without exception, are *victims;* but only believers can be *victors.*

No Threat from Within

Jesus himself makes this point absolutely clear. There is a story in Luke of our Lord's reaction to the challenge that was presented to him as he was casting out demons. This activity of our Lord, by the way, is an area of his ministry which is continually questioned by those who choose to approach the Scriptures intellectually. They do not like this business of casting out demons, and they explain it in various ways. We will say more about that later on, but in the biblical account certain ones said of Jesus that his ability to cast out demons came from his relationship with Beelzebub, the prince of demons—another name for Satan. They said it was by Satan's power, by Beelzebub's power, that he was casting out demons.

Beelzebub means "lord of the flies." The Jews regarded hell as a cosmic garbage dump, and in a real sense they were right, for that is exactly what hell is—a wasted life, a garbage dump. And because a garbage pile always attracts flies, they called Beelzebub the Lord of the Flies. These people were accusing Jesus of casting out demons by the authority of Beelzebub, the Lord of the Flies.

But Jesus said, "No, you are quite wrong. If that were true, then obviously Satan's kingdom would be divided against itself, and Satan would actually be pitted against the demons under his authority." Jesus states very simply that Satan never does that. Satan never fights against himself. He is too clever, too cunning, far too astute ever to divide his forces in that way, for he knows that if he did, his kingdom would fall. Jesus is suggesting, therefore, that any man who is under the control of Satan has no hope of deliverance apart from an outside, intervening force. Here is how he puts it: "When a strong man, fully armed, guards his own palace, his goods are in peace" (Luke 11:21). Who is the strong man? Satan. What is the palace? The world. Who are the goods? Mankind, everywhere. In the Luke 11:21-23 passage which presents this figure of the strong man there are three great principles which emerge. The first is that man alone against Satan is powerless and hopeless. This is the unchanging position of Scripture.

It is the position of the Bible that the world has fallen under the control of Satan. John says, "We [Christians] know that we are of God, and the whole world is in the power of the evil one" (1 John 5:19). Not the world of trees and mountains and lakes and seas—that is God's world—but the world of organized human society. It has fallen under the control of Satan, and there is no possibility of an escape apart from an intervention from without. For, as Jesus says, "When a strong man, fully armed, guards his own palace, his goods are in peace." There can be no threat from within to Satan's control.

It is just here that our Lord puts his finger on the reason for the continual failure of the usual methods men employ to correct evils and wrongs—the usual methods of reform. They fail because they do not come to grips with the essential problem. All our efforts to correct the evils we see in life are simply rearrangements of the difficulties. We succeed only in stirring them around a bit until they take a different form. But our methods can never solve the central problem of evil because they cannot come to grips with the power of Satan. As C. S. Lewis so aptly put it, "No clever arrangement of bad eggs will make a good omelet." When the full cycle of problems is run through, it begins again, and we say "history repeats itself."

Tried, But Not True

What are the usual methods of human reform? We can list them easily. Almost invariably they are *legislation, education,* and *an improved environment.* Every problem we face is usually approached by using one or a combination of these three. Legislation is law; it is merely the control of the outward man and has nothing to do with and cannot do anything to the inward man. It does not change the basic nature of man but merely restricts him under certain conditions.

Education is one of the worst so-called remedies for a deranged personality, a twisted mind. The position of Scripture is that all of us are born into this world with twisted minds. (Some are more twisted than others: they are the ones that *we* call "twisted minds"!) To educate a twisted mind is but to make it more clever in its wickedness. The educated criminal is a far more clever, more subtle, more difficult criminal to catch. The educated mind approaching human personality problems throws a shiny patina of knowledge over them which only serves to cover the real difficulties. Education does not basically change man; it only makes him more clever.

An improved environment does not change him, either. When you take a man out of the slums, for example, and put him into a nicer environment, you do absolutely nothing to the man himself. In a little while he will make that new environment a slum as well.

Now I do not mean to suggest that we scuttle these traditional approaches to reform. They all have certain values, but they do not come to grips with the basic problem. This is why, after a lifetime of trying to change man with these methods, those who are knowledgeable thinkers in this area always end up with a terribly black outlook on life. Listen to these words by Bertrand Russell, ". . . of whom," as a friend used to say, "there is none whomer," the high priest of the cult of freethinkers:

> *The life of man is a long march through the night, surrounded by invisible foes, tortured by weariness and pain, toward a goal that few can hope to reach and where none can tarry long. One by one as they march our comrades vanish from our sight, seized by the silent orders of omnipotent death. Brief and powerless is man's life. On him and all his race the slow, sure doom falls, pitiless and dark. Blind to good and evil, reckless of destruction, omnipotent matter rolls on its relentless way. For man, condemned today to lose his dearest, tomorrow himself to pass through the gates of darkness, it remains only to cherish, ere yet the blow falls, the lofty thoughts that ennoble his little day.*

Those eloquent words catalog the sheer despair into which man falls when he is far from God. There is a growing sense of despair everywhere you turn today. It is the unconscious realization of man's helplessness under Satan.

From Darkness to Light

Now look at the next verse and our Lord's words in Luke 11:22: "But when one stronger than he assails him and overcomes him, he takes away his armor in which he trusted, and divides his spoil." Who is this stronger one? It is Jesus. He is speaking of himself. He says when a strong man, fully armed, guards his palace, his goods are at peace and nothing can be done about it, least of all by the goods themselves. But when one who is stronger comes, he breaks the power of Satan. Here is the second principle the Lord is revealing in this passage, it is the good news of the gospel. We sing it:

> *He breaks the power of canceled sin,*
> *He sets the prisoner free;*
> *His blood can make the foulest clean,*
> *His blood availed for me.*

In the mystery of the cross of Jesus and in the power of his resurrection, applied by faith, we men and women who have been born into a society which is under the control of the satanic mind discover that the force which ruins us is broken and its power canceled.

That is why this Christian gospel is so exclusive. That is why Christians are perfectly justified when they say there is no other answer to the problems of man; there is no other power which can touch the basic problem of human life. There is only one "stronger one" who has come into the world and has come to grips with the power of this dark spirit and broken his power over human life.

How many there are who can testify to this throughout the Christian centuries! Not only prostitutes and alcoholics and dope addicts, not only those who have been gripped by the power of evil habits, but also those who have been held by the power of evil attitudes—temper, lust, self-righteousness, bitterness, and pride.

The strongest chains are not those around the

body, but around the mind. The writers of Scripture make that clear. In one place we read, "The god of this world has blinded the minds of the unbelievers" (2 Corinthians 4:4). And that great document on human liberty, the Epistle to the Romans, opens with that basic thought. Paul suggests that the greatest antagonism against the gospel does not come from the uneducated but from the educated—those who "thinking themselves wise, become fools," and change the glory of God into a lie.

But the gospel declares that Jesus Christ has come to set men free. John says Jesus came into the world "to destroy the works of the devil" (1 John 3:8). There is no adequate explanation of his coming apart from that. Paul says he has "delivered us from the dominion of darkness and transferred us to the kingdom of his beloved Son" (Colossians 1:13). Paul himself was chosen as an apostle to the Gentiles, and in that dramatic conversion experience on the Damascus road, he said to the Lord whom he saw in his glory, "What will you have me to do?" Jesus replied, "Stand upon your feet; for I have appeared to you for this purpose . . . delivering you from . . . the Gentiles—to whom I send you . . . that they may turn from darkness to light *and from the power of Satan to God*" (Acts 26:16-18).

This is what the gospel is for; it has no other purpose. If we try to channel it first into smaller areas of life, such as applying it to social concerns, we only reveal how far we have mistaken its purpose. The gospel will ultimately find its way there, certainly, but it must make its first impact upon this basic problem of human life. Mankind is in the grip of a power which it is helpless to do anything about. The only one who can deliver us from it is Jesus Christ. He has already done so in the mystery of his cross and through the power and glory of his resurrection.

When a person believes that and commits himself to Christ, he discovers that the gospel becomes practical in his own experience. This is what we call conversion. But conversion is only the beginning of the battle; very soon, a new Christian becomes aware of the evil forces at work to destroy him. If he goes no further in his new life than to believe his sins are forgiven, he will remain in bondage to those sins, living a life of conflict and frustration. But the battle is fought on the ground that we have been delivered from the dominion of darkness and brought out of the power of Satan into the kingdom of God.

The Crisis

Returning to the passage in Luke, we have seen, first, that man alone is helpless against the power of Satan. Next, our Lord speaks of the liberation that is available through belief in him, who has destroyed Satan's power. And finally, our Lord reveals one other principle in this passage: "He who is not with me is against me, and he who does not gather with me scatters" (Luke 11:23),. He is saying here that it is not possible to take a neutral stand and that mere profession is not sufficient. There are always those who say, "I understand something of the gospel, and I must confess that I believe there is much of value in the Christian faith. I am a friend of Christianity. I believe that it has a great moral impact to bring into our world, but I do not care to go so far as personally 'receiving Christ.' I think I will remain neutral."

Jesus says this is impossible. There is no neutrality. "He who is not with me is against me." He who has not received deliverance is still under the bondage and control of the dark powers of Satan. There are no exceptions.

This is why Christ is the crisis of history. He spoke of himself that way—as the divider of men. As he looks at men, there are only two groups. There are those who are wholly with him because they are of him—they have received him, know him, love him, and have partaken of his life. And there are those who are against him. "He who is not *with* me is against me."

On the other hand, some are tempted to say, "Well, if this is the case, then I want to be a Christian, but I don't know about all this inward control. I am willing to go along with the outward forms. I'm willing to join the church, but inwardly I still believe in directing my own life and running my own affairs." But Jesus says you cannot do that. "He who does not gather with me scatters."

There is one thing which will reveal whether you are with him or against him: the influence of your life. Jesus Christ has come into the world to gather together the children of God. His is a gathering influence, breaking down divisions, binding hearts together, reuniting families, making people to live together in harmony, breaking down the barriers of race, healing wounds, bringing nations together. But there is also a force which scatters, which divides. What is it? It is self-centeredness. This is the most divisive force known in human life. When people come together, the thing that splits them apart is their vested concern in their own affairs. They are self-centered.

Victor or Victim?

Therefore, the great question of life is What is basically the character of your life? Is it self-centeredness? Or is it self-givingness? Are you with him or against him? Are you gathering with him in a healing, wholesome ministry, or when you join a group, a family, an organization, a company, or a nation are you a divisive factor? Do you split people up? Do you cause them to quarrel with one another, come to odds with one another?

What about your own family? You say you are a Christian. All right. Are your children drawn closer to the faith because of you? Or are they breaking away from it because of you? Our Lord cuts right to the core of life. Life is absolutely laid bare and is judged finally on the basis of our relationship to him. The evidence of that relationship is the influence that we exercise.

The question each person must ask of himself is Am I a victor or a victim? Then we must realize that we are helpless to do anything about this ourselves. Nothing we can do in ourselves can change this situation. We are not free. We are not able to carry out our own decisions except in a limited area, and it is our illusion of freedom which makes us imagine that we are free, unrestrained individuals. According to the Bible, apart from Christ we are under the unbroken, absolute control of an evil force which is controlling our thoughts and reactions. And we are absolutely helpless to do anything about this until that power is broken by the acceptance of the One who has come to destroy the works of the devil.

If you have not known that deliverance you can know it now. Perhaps you have had to say, "If what you have said is true, then I am still an unbeliever. I am still under the power of Satan." Then the gospel comes to you now and this is its message: In one moment of time you can pass from death into life. In one moment of commitment, trusting Christ and his work, no longer reckoning upon anything you are trying to do to be good enough, you can say, "Lord, here am I. Save me." You pass in that moment from death into life. That is what conversion is. In those words you will open the door which permits him to do his saving work.

Our Father, may those who have been seeking for answers pass now from darkness into light, from the power of Satan into the kingdom of God, and be delivered, set free. For us, Lord, who have already experienced this and know something of the reality of this delivering power in our life, we pray that we may never forget that we have been set free, that Jesus did this for us when we could do nothing for ourselves. May we have a heart filled with love for him who loved us and gave himself for us. We pray in his name, amen.

3
THE STRATEGY OF SATAN

From beginning to end the picture given in the Bible is that all human beings, without exception, regardless of how clever or educated or cultured they may be, if without Christ are helpless victims of satanic control. Under the control of satanic forces human beings are uncomfortable and unhappy, but they are also completely unable to escape by any wisdom or power of their own.

But the good news is that some have been set free, some have been delivered. Through the coming of that "stronger one," Jesus himself, who came "to destroy the works of the devil," deliverance is obtained. Through the amazing mystery of the cross and the resurrection, Jesus has broken the power and bondage of Satan over human lives. Those who individually receive and acknowledge this (that is, those who believe, for Scripture always addresses itself to belief) are set free to live in the freedom and liberty of the children of God.

But they are not set free to live unto themselves. That is a common misconception. Many believe that Christ has come into their lives by means of the cross, and the things which have bound them and blasted them and ruined them have been stricken away, and they have been set free. But all too frequently they feel they have been set free to do as they please, to live as *they* want to live.

Not so; they are set free in order to battle. That is the call which comes to all Christians. We are not set free merely to enjoy ourselves. We are set free to do battle, to engage in the fight, to overcome in our own lives, and to become the channels by which others are set free.

We must now give closer attention to the actual conduct of the battle. If this conflict is the basic problem of human life, how much devolves upon us in conducting or fighting this battle? How do we accomplish this? Paul's answer is in one phrase: "Put on the whole armor of God." Full provision has been made for us to win the battle. This is the amazing truth we must learn. It is something we seldom take seriously—God has made full provision for us to fight these great and powerful forces which hold the world in their grip.

But it would be a mistake to begin our discussion with an examination of the armor of God. If we start there we find that this figure of armor strikes us with a note of unreality; it seems like a game. We shall end up talking about the armor of God, but we cannot start there. Rather, we must begin by seeing what it is we are opposed by. Armor is made for defense, and we will find no value in these pieces designed for our defense until we see what we are defending against. Let us realize something of the cleverness, the cunning wiliness of the forces against which we are battling, and we will begin to appreciate the armor with which we have been provided.

Armed with Cruel Hate

For now, I want primarily to look at this phrase of Paul's, "the wiles of the devil." The first step for any soldier in training is to be introduced to the strategy and weapons which the enemy will use against him. The devil is a very cunning and wily strategist. Martin Luther is quite right when he writes,

> *For still our ancient foe*
> *Doth seek to work us woe;*
> *His craft and power are great,*
> *And armed with cruel hate,*
> *On earth is not his equal.*

The record confirms this truth. Read the Old Testament and you will see that every saint, every prophet, every patriarch, every one of the great and glorious kings of Israel was defeated at one time or another by the devil. The wisest and greatest of men are absolutely helpless in attempting to outwit the devil by themselves. Yet as we have already seen, the Bible indicates that it is quite possible to walk in victory. James says, "Resist the devil and he will flee from you" (James 4:7). Think of that! This clever, cunning strategist who has held the world in defeat for centuries, whom no man is able to out-maneuver, will flee from you when you learn, like Paul, not to be ignorant of his devices.

Now, the questions we must ask are, What is the general strategy of the devil? How does he plan to do this? How is it that he keeps the world in such bondage? The only one in all history who has ever consistently defeated the devil, not only in his life but also in his death, is the Lord Jesus Christ. He put his finger squarely upon the strategy and the tactics of Satan when he said, "The devil is a liar and a murderer from the beginning" (John 8:44). The strategy of the devil is to murder. The tactic by which he accomplishes this is to lie. If we consider these phrases carefully, we will see how accurate they are.

How does the devil plan to oppose the work of God in the world? By murdering, by destroying. One of the names given to the devil in the Book of the Revelation is *Apollyon,* the Destroyer. What is it to destroy? It is to create chaos, to lay waste, to ruin, to make desolate. There you have the explanation for the whole tragic story of human history: A destroyer is at work among men. Our God is a God of beauty, harmony, order, and perfection, of love, of light, and grace. There is enough evidence left in the world of nature, including our own being, and in the world of ideas to see this marvelous symmetry, beauty, and perfection of God. God is a god of harmony and order. The world was created as orderly, and this includes man.

But then a destroyer came on the scene. It is his delight to smash, to mangle, to twist, to mutilate, to disfigure, to darken, and to blast in every way he can. It does not make any difference whether it is bodies or souls, flesh or ideas, matter or spirit, the aim of the devil is exactly the same in every case. That is why the devil can never offer anything positive to human life. He can make nothing. He has never made anything, and he never will make anything. All he can do is destroy what God has made. His power is totally negative, completely destructive in every way.

What are the tactics the devil employs? He destroys by deceiving, by lying, by distorting, by counterfeiting, by play-acting and masquerading, by illusion and fantasy. This is what Paul calls "the wiles of the devil." Read through the Bible and see how many times the work of the devil is referred to in that manner—the snares, the traps of the devil, the illusions, the strategems, the wiles. We shall content ourselves now with a general survey of these wiles, and in the next chapter we will take a much closer look at the actual tactics the devil is employing in your life and mine to defeat us and keep us in weakness, to ruin and lay waste our lives.

The Bible makes clear that the tactics of the devil fall into two major divisions. He attacks the human race both directly and indirectly. He is capable of a direct confrontation with human beings and an indirect approach. And through these two avenues he maintains his worldwide control over the race of men. The Bible indicates that there are fallen hosts of angels called demons, whom Paul refers to here as "the principalities and powers, the world rulers of this present darkness, the spiritual hosts of wickedness in heavenly places."

Now, *heavenly places* does not mean far off in heaven somewhere. *Heavenly* means "the realm of the invisibilities," the invisible realities of life. The devil and his hosts are not visible. The devil's activity is in this realm of the invisible reality of life, the heavenly places, where God also works.

Direct Assault

In the Bible we are told very little of the origin of the devil and his angels. But there is enough written to suggest that here was a being created originally as an angel of might and strength and beauty and power. There is a brief reference to the fall of this great angel, whose name was Lucifer, when he was lifted up by pride. Pride is always the mark of the devil. Lifted up by pride, he chose to rival God, and in doing so, he fell from his station of might and glory and beauty and became the devil (Isaiah 14:12-15; Luke 10:18). He drew a third of the angels with him, and these constitute the principalities and powers, the organized kingdom of darkness, as opposed to the kingdom of God. It is through these hosts of wicked spirits that Satan is able to make a direct assault upon human life.

This direct assault covers what the Bible refers to as "demonization," the outright control of human personality by the power of a wicked spirit. It also extends to such activities as soothsaying, occultism, spiritism (or spiritualism), and related black magic arts such as astrology, horoscopes, voodooism, fortune telling, and the like.

A word of warning is in order right here. There is no question that there is much chicanery and deception in this whole field of black magic. There are charlatans at work who make their living off the superstitious fears of people and who engage in deceptive tricks which give the impression they are genuinely dealing with the occult. It is very difficult to tell the difference between the genuine and the false in this field. Great care must be displayed by anyone attempting to investigate it. While there is a great deal of smoke, the Bible makes clear there is considerable fire as well. There is truth behind this black magic.

The Bible warns consistently against dabbling in these matters. Under the law the people of Israel were strictly forbidden to have anything to do with wizards "that peep and mutter," those who try to make contact with the dead or deal with the world of the occult. This prohibition was largely because any investigation into this realm immediately lays one open to powers beyond men's ken and makes possible control and influence beyond the will of the individual investigating. This is dangerous ground. In fact, it often opens the way to outright demonization.

As to this subject of demonization, I am very well aware there are many people who are incredulous. They say, "Surely you don't believe in that kind of stuff any more. In this twentieth-century day you're not telling us there are such things as demons! After all, the days in which the Bible was written were primitive times and people believed in that type of thing, but we're much better informed now. What was once called demon possession we now know to be only mental illness, and we can treat it with drugs and other therapy."

A Careful Distinction

What is our reply to that? Simply this: First, the Bible is not as primitive a book as many people imagine; it is very careful to distinguish between mental illness and demon possession. The writers of the Scriptures were certainly aware of this distinction. One of them, Luke, a physician himself, was certainly acquainted with the distinctions between physical diseases and mental illnesses and demon possession (Luke 4:40-41). In Matthew also, a careful distinction is made between those who were afflicted by diseases, those who were demon possessed, and those who were lunatic or mentally ill (Matthew 4:24).

Second, it is important to notice that the biblical

cases of demon possession do not conform to the clinical pattern of any known mental disease. There are
diseases of the body and there are diseases of the
mind. Diseases of the mind, like those of the body,
present standard clinical patterns which can be read-
ily recognized. But when you examine carefully the
biblical accounts of demon possession, you find these
do not fit any of the standard patterns of mental diseases. They are not the same thing; they do not conform.

In the first place, there is always a debasing element in the biblical cases of demonization, an uncleanness, a moral debasement. Also in the biblical
accounts of demonization there was an immediate recognition by the demon of the character and identity
of the Lord Jesus Christ. When Christ approached
these demons, many times they would call out,
"What have we to do with you, thou Son of God?"
They used titles for him which the victims they were
possessing were not at all acquainted with. There is
often this immediate and strange recognition of the
authority of Jesus Christ.

Further, there is always a totally distinct and different personality involved. In some cases many per-
sonalities were involved, as in the incident when
Jesus asked the name of the demon and the reply was,
"My name is Legion; for we are many" (Mark 5:9).
Finally, there is the ability on the part of Christ to
transfer demons from an individual to animals. How
do you explain the case of the Gadarene swine? If
demon possession is merely mental sickness, if it is
only hallucination, or if it is some kind of schizo-
phrenia, then how can the demons have left the man
and entered the swine, causing them to rush down
the hillside and drown themselves in the sea? These

cases simply do not conform to any clinical pattern of known mental disease.

A third factor is that Jesus himself invariably described these cases as demonization, and he treated them that way. In sending out his disciples he gave them authority to cast out demons. "Well," someone says, "we have an explanation for that. It is simply a recognition that Jesus was accommodating himself to the thought of the men of his day. They believed in demons and devils and he is simply speaking their language." But it is impossible to take that position and be consistent with the rest of the account of Christ's ministry, for we see him constantly correcting misconceptions like that. On one occasion he said to his disciples concerning another matter, "If it were not so I would have told you." He came to reveal the truth about things.

Throughout the Christian centuries there have been various outbreaks of demonization described by missionaries in many lands. It is a rather commonplace phenomenon in many places in our world today. And it is significant, I think, that wherever Christian teaching spreads, the direct assault of these evil powers upon human life is kept in abeyance. Even secular teaching which is based upon the Bible and Christian values and is moral and uplifting has an ability to keep these manifestations under control.

But when education becomes purely secular and denies the Bible and God, then even though men and women reject superstition and profess a degree of sophistication about these matters, it is not enough to keep these powers at bay. As our world grows more and more godless and more and more secularized, we will find an increasing tide of demonic manifestation creeping into our culture and insinuating itself into our civilized life. There is no power in man to with-hold these or to stand against them.

When Christians are confronted with what we sus-pect is demonization, the one thing we are told to do in order to help such people is to pray. These cases of demonization, Jesus said, yield to concerted and per-sistent prayer. Prayer is the recommended therapy in any case of this type. Let us give ourselves to prayer and nothing more.

For the sake of a balanced perspective, I must say I feel there is altogether too much concern among Christians about this matter of demonization. I know certain Christians who feel they must bind Satan be-fore they do anything. When they go into a room to have a meeting, they will pray to bind the powers of darkness. I know others who ascribe every common problem of human life to some manifestation of demon activity.

The New Testament gives absolutely no warrant for this type of approach. The apostles very seldom mention the direct attack of Satan against human be-ings. There are a few instances of it, but after our Lord physically left the world there seems to be a diminu-tion of the evidences of demonic activity. These dark powers were stirred up by his presence on earth, but to a degree this faded away after he left, so that in the epistles we do not find the same concern for demonic activity as we do in the gospels. There is much about Satan in the letters of Paul, but there is little of the direct attack of satanic forces. Nowhere do we read that Christians are instructed to go around binding the powers of darkness before we enter a room or that we are to ascribe all the common problems of life to demonic activities. The idea is not in the New Testa-ment.

By far, the majority of the attacks of the devil against Christians are not direct but indirect. That is why they are called the "wiles" of the devil. Wiliness means deviousness, circuitry, something not obvious. We need to examine this more thoroughly, for the major attack of the devil and his powers against human life is not by direct means, but indirect—by satanic suggestions through the natural and commonplace events of life.

Channels of Subversion

This indirect approach comes largely through two media or channels. One is what the Bible calls "the world," and the other, "the flesh." We often hear the idea, "The enemies of the Christian are the world, the flesh, and the devil," as though these were three equally powerful enemies. But there are not three. There is only one enemy, the devil, as Paul brings out in Ephesians 6. But the channels of his indirect approach to men are through the world and the flesh. Earlier in Ephesians, writing to Christians, the apostle says,

> *And you he* [that is, Christ, the "stronger one," who comes to set us free] *made alive, when you were dead through the trespasses and sins in which you once walked, following the course of this world* [there is the first channel, the world], *following the prince of the power of the air* [there is a description of the devil], *the spirit that is now at work in the sons of disobedience (Ephesians 2:1-2).*

He says, "Do not forget, you Christians, that you, too, once were following the course of this world—under the grip and in the control of the prince of the power of the air, the evil spirit which is now at work in all the children of disobedience." Further, he says,

> *Among these we all once lived in the passions of our flesh* [there is the flesh], *following the desires of body and mind* ["Oh," you say, "we were not aware of any control of the devil." No, of course not. You did what you felt like doing, the natural desires of the body and the mind. You responded to these so-called "natural" stimuli], *and so* [because we were doing these things, following the course of this world under the direction of the prince of the power of the air, and obeying the impulses of the body and the mind] *we were by nature children of wrath, like the rest of mankind (Ephesians 2:3).*

Do you see how consistently the Bible presents this picture? Now, the most basic of these two channels of approach to subverting the Christian life is the flesh. When the Bible speaks about the flesh, of course, the term is used in a symbolic sense. Many of us, when we approach middle age, are troubled with too much flesh! But that is not the sense in which the Bible uses the term. The flesh, in this context, is not our bodies, not the meat and blood and bones of our physical life. It is a term which describes the urge to self-centeredness within us, that distortion of human nature which makes us want to be our own god—that proud ego, that uncrucified self which is the seat of willful defiance and rebellion against authority.

You recognize that we are all born with this. None of us had to go to school to learn how to do these things. Who taught us to lie? Who taught us to be proud and bitter and rebellious and defiant and self-centered? We never had to take classes in these, did we? We were all experts in them by the time we were ready to go to school. We were all born with the flesh, and it is the presence of this which makes us sinners.

James calls this the wisdom which is from beneath, which is "earthly, unspiritual, devilish" (James 3:15). Devilish! It is the devil—attacking indirectly through the essential character of human nature, distorting it, twisting it, and changing it from what God intended. Paul says in Romans, as J. B. Phillips translates it, "Everyone has sinned, everyone falls short of the beauty of God's plan" (Romans 3:23).

The Kingdom of Satan

The world, on the other hand, is the corporate expression of all the flesh-centered individuals who make up the human race. Since the flesh is in every one of them—acting satanic, devilish, sensual, earthly—the total combined expression of such beings constitutes the world and determines the philosophy of the world. It is that tremendous pressure of the majority upon the minority to conform, adjust, keep in step, not to digress or to be different.

When the Bible addresses itself to Christians, it says, "Be not conformed to this world"; that is, "Do not let the world squeeze you into its mold." Why? Because the world is flesh-centered, flesh-governed, and as Jesus said to Nicodemus, "That which is born of flesh is flesh" (John 3:6). In order to be changed, it must be born of the Spirit. So this is the world—that human society which insists on satanic value judgments and is guided by satanic pride and philosophy. While the world is totally unaware of it, nevertheless it is under the control of satanic philosophy.

Remember this—the aim, the goal of Satan in all this clever strategem by which he has kept the human race in bondage through these hundreds of centuries is to destroy, to ruin, to make waste. That is his purpose toward you and me. A young man I know who had been raised in church, though he is only twenty-one years old has already become a mental and physical wreck. Why? Because he has turned aside from the truth and followed the philosophy of Satan. Satan is accomplishing his aim, destroying this life which God loves. That is what he is attempting to do with us all. Against this, we who are Christians are called to battle, not only for ourselves, as we will see in this account, but for others as well.

Battling against these forces of darkness is what makes human life possible on this earth. If Christians, who are the salt of the earth, were not giving themselves to an intelligent battle with Satan and satanic forces, fighting along these lines which Paul suggests—being "strong in the Lord and in the power of his might," it would be absolutely impossible for human life to exist on this planet. If this were not going on, life on earth would be one horrible, unending hell. It is the presence of Christians—and those who are affected by their testimony and by their teachings—and the spread of the gospel throughout the world which makes possible those moments of enjoyment of life which even the non-Christian is able to know.

> *We thank you, Father, that the victory is already won. Thank you for the privilege we have of moving over into the kingdom of God and for the chance to stop fighting a battle already lost and to begin fighting a battle already won. In Christ's name, amen.*

Finally, be strong in the Lord and in the strength of his might. Put on the whole armor of God, that you may be able to stand against the wiles of the devil. For we are not contending against flesh and blood, but against the principalities, against the powers, against the world rulers of this present darkness, against the spiritual hosts of wickedness in the heavenly places. Therefore take the whole armor of God, that you may be able to withstand in the evil day, and having done all, to stand (Ephesians 6:10-13).

4
THE TACTICS
OF TERROR

Some time ago I heard of a mental hospital that had devised an unusual test to determine when patients were ready to go back into the world. They brought any candidates for release into a room where a tap was turned on and water was pouring out over the floor. Next they handed the patient a mop and told him to mop up the water. If the patient had sense enough to turn off the tap before mopping up the water, he was ready to go out into society. But if, as in the case of many, he started mopping up the water while the tap was still running, they knew more treatment was needed.

When we laugh at that, I am afraid we are laughing at ourselves, because that is what many of us are doing. Each Christian, facing the personal world in which he lives, is given the mop of truth and told to use it. But we can only help in that world if we have enough intelligence to conquer first the evil which is pouring into our own hearts from these world rulers of present darkness.

That is exactly what the apostle Paul is urging in Ephesians 6:10-13. We can be of no possible help in the solutions of world problems as long as we remain part of the problem. Therefore this whole passage is designed to awaken us and to call our attention to the need for understanding the nature of our problem. As we have seen, it is through the channels of the world and the flesh that the devil makes his indirect and most insidious attack upon human life. The "world" is human society, blindly and universally accepting false values, shallow concepts and insights, and deluded ideas of reality. At the same time it almost desperately insists upon conformity to those standards and insights. The flesh is that urge within us toward total independence, toward being our own little gods and running our worlds to suit ourselves. It is that continual drift within us toward self-centeredness and selfishness that keeps us from being completely God's.

You can see immediately that the struggle against the influences of the world and the flesh is not something remote from us, nor something which occasionally comes to a certain few Christians. This is a battle in which we are all engaged every moment of our lives because the flesh, this inner arena of battle, accompanies us everywhere we go. We cannot escape it, we cannot run away from it. Therefore we must begin our battle at this point.

But someone says, "I thought that when you become a Christian, Christ sets you free from the kingdom of Satan, and the devil no longer can touch you—that you have nothing to do with the devil anymore." Is that your concept of the Christian life? Nothing could be more wrong! When you become a Christian, the battle only begins.

Miserable Christians

It is true the devil can never totally defeat a Christian. Those who are genuinely the Lord's, who are born again, who have come into a saving relationship with Jesus Christ, are delivered from total defeat. We do not hesitate to emphasize that! The devil can never get us back into the position of unconscious control which he once exercised over us, as he does over the rest of the world. But the devil *can* demoralize the Christian. He can frighten us, make us miserable, and defeat us in many ways. He can make us weak and barren and unfruitful in the things of God. It is quite possible, at least occasionally, to be more miserable as a Christian than you ever were before.

The devil is especially interested in defeating Christians. After all, the unredeemed worldling is no problem to him. All the quite sincere but rather pathetic efforts of worldlings to solve the problems of their lives through legislation, education, and a change of environment do not bother the devil in the least. He is quite content to let them go on rearranging the pieces of the puzzle without ever solving it. But the presence of every Christian in this world bothers the devil greatly. Why? Because each Christian is a potential threat to the solidarity of the devil's kingdom, to his rule over the rest of mankind.

If the devil did not oppose the Spirit of God, every individual Christian, without exception, would be a powerful force to destroy the devil's kingdom of darkness. Each Christian would be to others a door of escape out of the unconscious control of these world rulers of present darkness. Every Christian would be a corridor of liberty, a center of light, dispelling the darkness and ignorance of the world around him.

The devil cannot let that happen if he can help it, so he attacks the Christian, especially and particularly. He marshals all his forces against us, coming sometimes as a "roaring lion" in some catastrophic circumstance which seems to knock us off our feet. At other times he comes as "an angel of light," alluring, appealing, offering something that seems to be just the right thing for the right moment. Or he will take over the direct control of human life whenever he can. Thus we find men like Hitler arising on the world scene from time to time, demonic men motivated by strange and unexplainable passions. Sometimes the devil assails us through the world with its monstrous pressure to keep in line, not to be different, and with its ostracism of those who attempt to swim against the stream. But most often the devil comes in disguise, through the channel of the flesh—our inner selves—with silken, subtle, suggestive wiles. That particularly is what the apostle is warning against—the wiles of the devil.

We must now take a closer look at this flesh within us. According to the Bible, the flesh, in this symbolic sense, is identified with the body which ultimately dies. In Romans Paul says, "your bodies are dead because of sin" (Romans 8:10). We would say, "The body is dying because of sin," but the apostle looks on to the end and says that it is as good as dead already. We all agree with this. "We all must die," we say.

In this temporary state before the resurrection, the body is the seat of sin or the flesh—this evil principle of self-centeredness in each of us. Therefore the flesh is going to be with us for life. We may as well face that. We are never going to get away from it. We shall never escape it until that wonderful day of the resurrection from the dead. The body is dead because of sin, and we live with it, therefore, for life.

The Devil's Access

But the body, soul, and spirit of man are inextricably tied together. No one can understand this. Where does your soul live in your body? Do you know? No, but you know that you have a soul, though no one can locate it in the body. The relationship between the body, soul, and spirit is beyond our comprehension. But because they are so inextricably tied together, the flesh, linked to the body, touches the whole man. It is important to see this. This means that the devil can influence us in the body, in the soul, and in the spirit. He has access to the whole man through the channel of the flesh. Put another way, we are subject to the influence of these world rulers of present darkness through our mind, our feelings, and our deeds—through our intelligence, our emotions, and our will. We need to see how this works. Through the channel of the mind—the intellect—the devil makes his appeal to human pride. Through the channel of emotions, he works on human fears, and in the realm of deeds—the things we choose to do or say—the devil makes his appeal to pleasure, since we are essentially sensuous beings.

See how accurately this is illustrated by the story of Eve in the Garden of Eden. We are told that when she saw that the fruit was good for food—it offered the pleasant sensation of eating (the appeal to the body) —and it was a delight to the eyes—awakening within her a sense of beauty (the appeal to the emotions)—and when she saw that it was desired to make one wise—the appeal to the pride of mind, the appeal to intelligence and love of wisdom—she took and ate. These are simply the channels by which men are moved, whether by God or the devil. This is the way men are. Both of the forces outside man which work upon man, God and the devil, move him through these channels: the emotion—the heart; the mind— the intelligence; and the will—the power to choose.

Well, you say, if the devil and God both move us by the same channels, what is the difference? The difference is simply this: The devil moves to create an imbalance, an eccentricity. The devil is the original extremist. God moves, however, toward balance, harmony, and beauty. The difference is not how they work, but the direction in which they move.

A Sanity of Balance

The greatness of the gospel is in its appeal to the whole man, to the whole of life. It is this fact tha reveals its divine origin so clearly. The gospel touches and explains all of history. It has a world view, and i provides a framework for every science, every endeavor to investigate, every event of history.

The gospel is not content simply to adjust a few problems in man. We often come to Christ asking him to resolve some immediate difficult situation in which we find ourselves. But he never stops there. He knows us, and he knows that if he solves this small problem here or that small problem there he has touched only a part of our life and the rest will remain out of balance, eccentric. So the gospel makes its appeal to the whole of man and touches every part of his life.

You can see this in the life of our Lord. Read the gospel records and see what a marvelous balance there is in the Lord Jesus, what perfect poise he exhibits in every circumstance. He says things which absolutely challenge the greatest thinkers of his time, and they listen with astonishment to his words and insights. Some of them said, "No man every spoke like this man."

But he is not all intellect, making his appeal to the philosopher alone. As you read the record, you see that he is also warmly human. He is constantly expressing compassion and human concern. He is easy to live with. Further, Jesus manifests both intelligence and emotionalism through his deeds. He is not content merely to feel certain things or to talk about certain great truths, but these find their ultimate expression in practical deeds, in actions—in unforgettable, undeniable events such as the cross and the resurrection.

You can see this wonderful appeal to the whole of man in the Scriptures. What a marvelous sanity of balance is maintained in the Bible! The whole man is ministered to—the needs of the soul, the body, and the spirit—all kept in a delicate equilibrium with nothing out of balance. Everything is in harmony— the mind, the heart, and the will are all moved together. When God gets hold of a man, he begins to touch every part of his life. Anything less is an incomplete message, a mere fragment.

I am indebted to Dr. Martin Lloyd-Jones for pointing out that this is beautifully expressed in one of the familiar hymns of Isaac Watts: "When I Survey the Wondrous Cross."

When I survey the wondrous cross,
On which the Prince of Glory died . . .

To begin with, my mind is engaged when I think about the cross, when I give intelligent consideration to what it means, when I think of all that was involved in that supreme hour when Jesus hung between heaven and earth. When I survey the wondrous cross on which the Prince of Glory died—my intelligence is captured. I see there are deep and marvelous things about this event. And then what? Well, it moves my emotions:

My richest gain I count but loss,
And pour contempt on all my pride.

I am moved, my emotions are immediately involved. I have learned that when people talk about the truth of the Word and it does not move them emotionally, they have not really understood the truth. Truth is designed to reach the heart to move it and to involve it. As you go on in this song, you see how marvelously the emotions are involved:

Were the whole realm of nature mine,
That were a present far too small . . .

Here is a sense of the grandeur of the work of the cross, the extent of it, and the glory of it.

Love so amazing, so divine . . .

Love does what? Demands! There is the will being impelled to action:

Demands my soul, my life, my all.

The whole man is totally engaged. That is the way God works!

Grotesque Caricatures

But what does the devil do? Well, he tries to create imbalance—to build up one element of man's nature at the expense of others, to push us to an extreme, to turn us into persons who are characterized by only one thing. Instead of whole persons, we are grotesque caricatures of men.

There are many who take pride in emphasizing one part of their being above everything else. First, there are the intellectuals—we call them "eggheads," "brains." They say there is nothing important in life but the mind, the ability to reason, and they give themselves to the development of this area of life. As a result, they are so absentminded, so impractical, one can hardly live with them! Because they are out of balance we call them eccentric.

Then there are the emotional people, those who say, "Oh, don't talk to me about intellectual things. I have no patience with that. I want to experience life, to feel it, and to enter into things." These people are always living on their feelings, their emotions. Sometimes we call them "empty headed" because they never seem to use what is in their heads. These are the people who, when you ask them what they think, say, "How do I know what I think until I've heard what I have to say?" Or they are introverted, always feeling around inside, endlessly examining themselves. There is nothing wrong with self-examination; it is very much a part of the Christian life. But these people never do anything else. They are constantly looking at themselves, morbidly examining themselves, and expressing gloom over what they find.

Then, of course, there are those who say, "I have no

patience with the thinker or with the feeler. I'm a man of practicality." "Hardheaded," we call them, involved only in deeds and concerned only with practical matters. "What do you do?" is always the issue with them. All three of these extremes are wrong. They are unbalanced—not what God intends man to be. It is the devil who pushes us into these extremes. It is the devil who takes each of these elements and tries to get us off balance within them.

Take the realm of mind, for instance. Through the wiles of the devil we are encouraged to exalt reason to the exclusion of faith. Faith is a function of the will, the soul. That is why faith is the most human characteristic of man—because it is a function of the soul—that element of man which is our basic motivator. That is why everyone can exercise faith. You are not human, you are not even alive, if you cannot exercise faith. But the devil tries to move from a balance in this area by appealing to our pride. We love to think of ourselves as logicians, justifying everything we do on the basis that it is a logical development of a certain premise we have taken. But this exaltation of reason opens the door to error and deceit.

One of the great examples of this, which we are hearing a good deal about these days, is the teaching in popular books and elsewhere that the Bible is too primitive. It no longer makes its appeal to "grown-up man," to "man come of age." These descriptive phrases make their subtle appeal to the pride of intellect: "man come of age"; "twentieth century man!"

The Bible, the thesis goes, offends the integrity of modern man, strains his credulity. We can no longer accept it as a historical record; it is simply the attempt on the part of the early church to express things in mythical form. These things did not really happen but are reported as though they happened in order that we might get the great truth behind them. Man "come of age" does not worry about the worm in which truth comes, but about the truth itself.

Continuing this line of thought, man come of age needs to have a new concept of God. Man needs to understand God in a different light. What is this new concept? What is this amazing insight to which mature man has come, through the difficult struggle of the ages, having finally grown up and become able to see something new about God? What is it? Well, it is that God is no longer the Father, as our Lord Jesus pictured him (which in one book is ridiculed as "the Old Man in the Sky" concept). God is not a Father in that sense. The new idea is that God is the "Ground of our Being." If you really want to be an intelligent man, if you want to understand what this whole business of Christianity has been driving at all along, then move on to this new concept of God—he is the Ground of our Being! This theme has been offered as if it were a revolutionary advance in theological thinking.

The fact is, this idea presents the most primitive concept about God. Turn to the story of the apostle Paul's journey to the center of intellectualism of his day—the city of Athens—and read his great address to the Athenians on Mars Hill. As he walked around the city, he found evidences of a superstitious, ignorant, and pagan faith everywhere he went . . . even finding an altar that was addressed "To an Unknown God." He said to them, "What therefore you worship as unknown, this I proclaim to you" (Acts 17:23). He started on that level.

He said, "Look, you know yourselves that God does not dwell in temples made of stones—not the God who made the heavens and the earth and all things that are in them. Your own poets have recognized the fact that God is not far from any one of us, for in him we live and move *and have our being.*" They already knew that much about God. That is the simplest level of faith—primitive faith, the faith which is the result of an ignorant searching and groping after God. But it is through such teaching as I have been describing that the devil cleverly succeeds in pushing the mind of man, through an appeal to his pride, out to what he thinks are new advances but in reality are nothing more than a simple and primitive understanding of God.

In the realm of the mind, the devil is constantly trying to create doubt. Here he plants his heresies and incites false teaching. False teaching always takes an extreme position, exaggerating one particular aspect of truth and blowing it up out of proportion—extremism. That is one of the devil's favorite maneuvers. He does this even about himself in trying to make people believe there is no devil. After all, isn't concealment an essential ploy in trying to capture some wild animal? You try to hide yourself; you do not want to be seen. This is what the devil does. He persuades people that there is no such thing as the devil. Then he is perfectly free to do exactly what he wants to do with humanity.

But if someone wakes up and refuses to believe that, then the devil comes and says, "You're perfectly right! Of course there is a devil. You know it and I know it. But my power, my cunningness, my strategy, and my wiliness are so great that you had better give all your time and thought in an effort to overcome me!" Thus he pushes some over to another extreme which will lead on to superstition, voodooism, and other fear-related positions.

With Christians, the devil often works in the realm of the mind to get us over-concerned with certain points of theology. There are those Christians who pride themselves on being Bible students and who know all the ins and outs of theology. They wander through all the dark woods of theological differences and climb the icy peaks of various doctrines, such as predestination and the decrees of God. For them, all that matters is doctrine. Or perhaps it is prophecy, or Bible numerics—they get so involved studying the numbers of the Bible that they end up using a computer for their Bible study.

An Appeal to Fear

Now the realm of feelings yields a prolific area for satanic attack. We are used to believing our feelings. From babyhood we have been used to reacting to the way we feel and accepting the way we feel as a legitimate and accurate description of the way things are. Nothing could be more foolish. There is nothing that is more uncertain and more unrealistic than our feelings. Most of the time they do not relate to reality at all because they are subject to so many influences.

The devil moves some Christians to live on a plane of exhilaration, of constant joy. When they get together, their meetings are a riot of handclapping, shouting, and religious joy—or perhaps more accurately a religious jag. Often he pushes to the opposite extreme. They think to express happiness as a Christian marks them as sinful. They are all gloom and introspection, morbidity. Or the devil leads people to shift from one to another—one time they are up and the next moment they are down, one day they are up on top and the next day, because of their feelings, they are down in the depths. They live on an emotional teeter-totter. If this describes you, then you have already succumbed to the wiles of the devil.

This is what keeps some people defeated. The devil

gets them exercised about being concerned and showing compassion to the point that they are acutely anxious all the time, filled with worry and fretful com-
plaint. But when they see that is wrong, then he
blandly seeks to push them over to the other side and
they become callous and cynical, not caring for any-
body. The devil always makes his appeal in this realm
to our fears while God makes his appeal to faith.
From faith comes hope and love, but the devil wants
us to give way to our fears.

The one thing Jesus said over and over again to his
disciples was, "Fear not. Be not fearful, be not anxious, be not troubled." Why? Because "I am with
you," he said. From fear comes despair, the opposite
of hope, and hate, the opposite of love. That is what
the devil is after. If you give way to fear, you will soon
be discouraged and defeated. If you give way to defeat, you will begin to hate and the devil will have
accomplished his purposes. He has destroyed, he has
ruined, he has laid waste that which God loves and
desires to bless.

In the realm of deeds, the devil works to get some
to seek a continual round of something new, something exciting—appealing to their desire for continu-
ous pleasure in activities. We have to be constantly
satisfied with some exciting activity. The devil
pushes others in the opposite direction, into a rut
called "tradition," which they fiercely defend. They
say, "These people that are forever running after new
things! Not for me. I want the same things for break-
fast every morning, for lunch every day, for supper
every night. I come home at the same time, I read the
same page of the same paper at the same hour of the
day." Everything is the same; thus they avoid any
painful adjustments to change in their lives.

God never intended life to be lived that way or the

other way. God's will for man represents a great highway right through the center of life where the whole man is ministered to. That is where the Lord Jesus walked and that is where the Scriptures take us, if we walk by them.

Now, we've made just a brief survey of this subject. I have said almost nothing about the devil's attack through the world, with its illusions, its allures, and its pressures to conform—"Everybody does it, you know." The devil gets us that way, too. But that is why we have the Scriptures, that is why the Word of God is given to us—that it might instruct us in all the ways of evil. No wonder we do not escape if we will not give ourselves to an understanding of these.

But perhaps I have said enough to make you ask yourself, "Who is sufficient for these things? How can we possibly understand all this? Who can hope to win against such a variety of attacks? Who can even grasp, let alone answer, these subtle and powerful attacks against human life?" Does it leave you feeling rather discouraged? If it does, then look once more at what Paul is saying here. His word to us is: "Finally, be strong in the Lord and in the strength of his might. Put on the whole armor of God, that you may be able to stand against the wiles of the devil."

You see, there is a provision. Perhaps the most healthy attitude we can have in the face of this revelation is to be overpoweringly aware of our sense of weakness. It is when we recognize we are weak that we are ready to "be strong in the Lord and in the strength of his might," ready to give intelligent consideration to what that is and how to do it.

Teach us, Father, to have the humility to admit that we have not been doing a very good job on this score, and that we have been snared time and time again by the wiles of the devil. Lord, grant to us a willingness to listen, to give careful, thoughtful, and continued attention to the way of victory provided through Jesus Christ our Lord, who has known all along that we would face this kind of battle and has been trying to tell us, but we have been so slow of hearing. Lord, make us attentive to his word. In Christ's name we pray, amen.

Stand therefore, having girded your loins with truth, and having put on the breastplate of righteousness, and having shod your feet with the equipment of the gospel of peace; besides all these, taking the shield of faith, with which you can quench all the flaming darts of the evil one. And take the helmet of salvation, and the sword of the Spirit, which is the word of God (Ephesians 6:14-17).

5
INTO THE
ARMORY

The goal of the devil is always to produce discouragement, confusion, or indifference. Wherever we find ourselves victims of a state of confusion and uncertainty, or discouragement and defeat, or an indifferent and callous attitude toward life or others, we have already become prey to the wiles of the devil. But this need not be so. The Ephesians passage we are studying describes God's adequate defense against the devil's tactics, and we are urged and encouraged to use it. "Be strong in the Lord," the apostle says, "and in the strength of his might." It is possible to stand; it is possible to overcome.

But although this word is very encouraging to us,

it alone is not enough. It tells us there is an answer, but it does not tell us exactly what it is. Our question always is, How do you do this? How, exactly, do you become strong in the Lord and in the strength of his might?

The Armor Is Christ

The answer is, "Put on the whole armor of God." That is how to become strong in the Lord and in the strength of his might. Paul says,

> *Stand therefore, having girded your loins with truth, and having put on the breastplate of righteousness, and having shod your feet with the equipment of the gospel of peace; besides all these, taking the shield of faith, with which you can quench all the flaming darts of the evil one. And take the helmet of salvation, and the sword of the Spirit, which is the word of God (Ephesians 6:14-17).*

You can see this is highly figurative language. These are not entities in themselves but symbols of something real. In order to understand them we must look behind the figures to the reality. The armor is the way to be strong in the Lord and in the strength of his might. The armor is nothing more than a symbolic description of the Lord himself. The armor is Christ and what he is prepared to be and to do in each one of us. When Paul speaks of these various pieces of armor, he is speaking of Christ and how we are to regard him—how we are to lay hold of him as our defense against the stratagems of the devil. It is not merely Christ available to us, but Christ actually appropriated.

In Romans Paul clearly declares this concept: "Put on the Lord Jesus Christ, and make no provision for the flesh, to gratify its desires" (Romans 13:14). Also, writing to his son in the faith, the apostle says to Timothy, "You then, my son, be strong in the grace *that is in Christ Jesus*" (2 Timothy 2:1). That is the source of our armor. Christ is our defense. Therefore we need to study this armor in order to learn how to lay hold of Christ in a practical way.

General truth, I have discovered, does not help us very much. It is easy to speak in empty generalities about Christian living. Sometimes we pick a phrase out of Scripture and employ it almost as an incantation or some kind of magic defense. But that is a grossly improper use of the Bible.

It is easy for us to say glibly to some Christian who is struggling through a difficult time, "Christ is the answer!" Well yes, Christ *is* the answer, but *how* is he the answer? That is what we need to know, and this is what the armor in our text describes. Jesus Christ is the answer as a specific defense against specific things.

Before we look at the armor more precisely, there are two things we must note which are brought out in this text. First, there are two general divisions or classifications of the pieces of armor, and these are indicated by the tenses of the verbs which are used. The first division, covering the first three pieces, is something we have already done in the past if we are Christians: "*having girded* your loins with truth"; "*having put on* the breastplate of righteousness"; "*having shod* your feet with the equipment of the gospel of peace." The second division includes those things which are to be put on or taken up at the present moment: "*taking* the shield of faith"; "*take* the helmet of salvation, and the sword of the Spirit." We are to take up these aspects of Christ which we take up again and again whenever we feel under attack.

The second thing to note about this armor as it is

described in the text is the order in which these pieces
are given to us. You cannot alter the order in any way.
For example, the reason many Christians fail to exercise the sword of the Spirit is that they have never first
girded up their loins with truth. You cannot do it in
reverse order; Scripture is very exact in this.

Tuck Up the Tunic

Now we want to look at the first three items which
constitute the first division of this armor: "Having
girded your loins with truth"—that is always the
place to start whenever you are under attack.
Whenever you feel discouraged, defeated, uncertain,
confused, downcast, depressed, or indifferent, this is
the place to start: "Gird up your loins with truth."

The officers in the Roman army wore short skirts
very much like Scottish kilts. Over them they had a
cloak or tunic which was secured at the waist with a
girdle. When they were about to enter battle they
would tuck the tunic up under the girdle so as to leave
their legs free and unimpeded for the fight. Girding
the loins was always a symbol of readiness to fight.
That is why this is first. You cannot do battle until
you first gird up your loins with truth.

When you are threatened by discouragement, cold-
ness, and similar moods, how do you fight back? You
are to remember that when you became a Christian
you girded up your loins with truth. What does that
mean precisely? It means to remind yourself that in
coming to Jesus Christ you found the truth behind
all things, you found him who is in himself the truth,
the key to life, the secret of the universe, final reality!
You find the truth used in that sense earlier in this
same letter: "You did not so learn Christ! [that is, in
uncleanness and licentiousness, etc.]—assuming

that you have heard about him and were taught in him, as the truth is in Jesus" (Ephesians 4:20-21).

He is the truth, he is reality, he is the key to life, "in whom are hid all the treasures of wisdom and knowledge" (Colossians 2:3). "Well," someone says, "how do you know that? You say you believe in Jesus, but you have accepted him as the authority without any evidence to support it. That's blind faith." But everyone begins with an act of faith, accepting some principle or person as the final authority in life. It is either another religious leader or a principle such as a scientific method or perhaps nothing more than "what I feel is right."

The distinctive thing about Christianity is that Jesus Christ has more clearly demonstrated the right to be accepted as that authority than anyone else or any other principle. The Christian therefore bets his life, in a sense, that Jesus Christ is the real authority, the true revelation of things as they really are. He has objectively demonstrated it and subjectively confirmed it to you as a Christian.

Faith Informed

How did he demonstrate that he was the truth? First, by what he said. Read the things he said—incomparable things! He gave the clearest insights ever offered in the hearing of men as to what human life is all about. Even his enemies say so. No one ever saw so clearly as he, no one ever probed so deeply or put his finger so precisely upon the elements which make up human life and thinking. It is clear in what Jesus said that he spoke the truth.

But beyond that, he demonstrated the truth by what he did. This New Testament record is an amazing account of mighty deeds and historic events. Miracles?

Yes, there are evidences of the intrusion of the spiritual kingdom—that invisible realm of reality—into the visible realm. And he capped it all, of course, by showing that he had solved the one problem which is insoluble to every other man—the problem of death. He rose from the dead! Who else has ever done anything like that? That is why I know Jesus Christ is the truth—because he solved the problem of death.

This, by the way, is why the enemies of the Scriptures fight so fiercely to destroy the historicity of these events. They want us to think it does not matter whether these were historically true. Of course they are historically true, and of course it greatly matters, for these events demonstrate that Jesus is the truth.

But it is not only by what he said and by what he did that we can know he is the truth. We can know by what he is now, in this present day. What has he been to you? What has he been to others? Look back at your own Christian life and its beginnings. Did he deliver you? Has he set you free? Has he broken any chains in your life? Has he been your friend? Has he brought you back into balance and harmony?

It has been pointed out that through the centuries men have been calling on others to help. You may lack courage and say, "John F. Kennedy, help me!" but nothing happens. You may lack wisdom and ask, "Winston Churchill, help me!" Or lacking eloquence, you may cry, "Shakespeare, help me!" But no help comes. Yet for twenty centuries men and women in desperate plight have been calling out, "Lord Jesus Christ, help me!"—and help is given! Deliverance comes! That is how we know he is the truth.

Remember that all conflicting systems and philosophies must be tested at all points, not at just one. Many philosophies can do something; many systems which basically are wrong can still help in a limited area. They can help somewhere and accomplish some good. But this is never the mark of truth. Truth is a complete entity. Truth is reality—the way things really are. Therefore it is the explanation of all things. You know you have found the truth when you find something which is wide enough and deep enough and high enough to encompass all things. And that is what Jesus Christ does.

Further, ultimate reality never changes. Here is another mark. Truth never requires updating, never needs to be modernized. If something was true ten thousand years ago, it is still true today. If it is true today, it was true a hundred thousand years ago.

I delight in the story of the man who came to his old friend, a music teacher, and said to him in the flippant way we moderns use, "What's the good news today?" The old man never said a word. He walked across the room, picked up a hammer, and struck a tuning fork. As the note sounded out through the room, he said, "That is *A*. It is *A* today, it was *A* five thousand years ago, and it will be *A* ten thousand years from now. The soprano upstairs sings off-key, the tenor across the hall flats his high notes, and the piano downstairs is out of tune." He struck the note again and said, "That is *A*, my friend, and that's the good news for today!"

Jesus Christ is unchanging. He is the same yesterday, today, and forever. That is how you know you have truth. Remember that when you feel defeated, when you are under attack, when doubts come flooding into your mind. Remember that you have girded up your loins with truth; you have found him who is the solid rock. "On Christ the solid rock I stand, all other ground is sinking sand."

Security Guard

Now look at the second piece of armor—the breast-plate of righteousness. Have you put that on? "Having put on the breastplate of righteousness"—what does that mean? Well, that is Christ as the ground of your righteous standing before God, your acceptance before him. If you have the breastplate of righteousness on, you can rest secure that your heart and your emotions are perfectly guarded and adequately protected against attack.

Christians, through one circumstance or another, often lack assurance; they feel unworthy of God. They feel they are a failure in the Christian life and that God, therefore, is certain to reject them, that he is no longer interested in them. Christians are so aware of their failures and short-comings. Growth has been so slow. The first joy of faith has faded, and they feel God is angry with them or that he is distant. There is a constant sense of guilt. Their conscience is always stabbing them, making them unhappy and miserable. They feel God blames them. This is simply a satanic attack, a means of opposing and destroying what God intends to do.

How do you answer an attack like this? You are to remember that you have put on the breastplate of righteousness. In other words, you do not stand on your own merits. You never did. You never had anything worthwhile in yourself to offer to God. You gave all that up when you came to Christ. You quit trying to be good enough to please God. You came on *his* merits. You came on the ground of his imputed righteousness—that which he gives to you. You began your Christian life like that, and *there is no change now*. You are still on that basis.

This is why Paul begins his great eighth chapter to

the Romans with the words, "There is therefore now no condemnation for those who are in Christ Jesus" (Romans 8:1). No condemnation! You are believing a lie when you believe that God is angry with you and that he rejects you. Remember, you stand on Christ's merits, "accepted in the Beloved." Further on in that chapter Paul asks, "Who can accuse us?" It is God who justifies. Christ, who died for us, is the only one who has the right to accuse us, and he loves us. Therefore there is no separation. "Who can separate us from the love of God in Christ Jesus?" Who can do this?

This does not mean, of course, that God puts his hand on the things we know are wrong in our lives and says, "Oh well, these things don't matter. Don't worry about them." But it means he sees them and says, "Oh, yes, but he hasn't learned yet all that I intend to teach him." And he deals with us as a father in love and patient discipline—as a father, not as a judge.

See how the apostle Paul himself used this breastplate of righteousness when he was under pressure to be discouraged and defeated. Have you ever thought of the struggles he personally had in this realm? Here was a man who was small of stature, unimpressive in his personal appearance—in fact, there is very good evidence to indicate that he was even repulsive to many. He had a disfiguring physical ailment which made him unpleasant to look at. The last thing he had was what is called a commanding presence.

Paul's background was anti-Christian, and he could never get completely away from that. He had been the most hostile, brutal persecutor the church had known. He must have constantly run across families with loved ones whom he had put to death. And he was often reminded by many people that he was not one of the original twelve apostles, that his calling was suspect, that perhaps he really was not an apostle at all. Writing to the Corinthians about these very matters, he says of himself, "I am the least of the apostles, unfit to be called an apostle, because I persecuted the church of God" (1 Corinthians 15:9).

What grounds for discouragement! How easy it would have been for him to say to himself, "What's the use? Here I am working my fingers to the bone, making tents and trying to preach the gospel to these people, and look at the blessing God has brought them, but they don't care. They hurl recriminations back into my face. What's the use? Why try any more?"

But that is not what he does. The very next verse says, "By the grace of God I am what I am, and his grace toward me was not in vain" (1 Corinthians 15:10). There he is using the breastplate of righteousness. I don't care, he says, what I have been. I don't defend what I am. I simply say that by the grace of God I am what I am. What I am is what Christ has made me. I'm not standing on my righteousness, I'm standing on his. I am accepted by grace, and my personal situation does not make any difference at all.

So his heart was kept from discouragement. He could say, "Sure, all these things are true, but that does not change the fact that I am Christ's man, and I have his power. He is in me and I can do all things through Christ who strengthens me." Thus he reminded himself that when he became a Christian he had put on the breastplate of righteousness, and he never allowed himself to be discouraged, for he never looked back for anything. He looked to Christ.

A Stout Pair of Shoes

Now let us look at this third piece of armor—"Having shod your feet with the equipment of the gospel of peace." Shoes are absolutely essential to fighting. Imagine a soldier clad in armor from head to foot but with no shoes on—a barefoot soldier. Imagine how quickly the rough ground would tear and bruise his feet. Soon, despite the fact that he had all the equipment he needed otherwise, he would be out of combat. His feet would render him unfit to fight. But with a stout pair of shoes he would be ready and equipped, able to fight.

That is what this phrase means. "Equipment" here is really the word "readiness" in Greek. "Your feet shod with the readiness produced by the good news of peace." It is peace in the heart that makes you able to fight. What does this mean? Well, again it is Christ, but this time it is Christ our peace, our source of calm, the one who provides a sense of well-being.

Now notice the relation of one piece of armor to another and the importance of the order that I stressed earlier. The first piece tells us that Christ is the truth, the ultimate secret of reality. We have come home; we have touched the key to life in Jesus Christ. That is something for the mind to understand and grasp and believe.

And then what? Well, we know Christ then. We stand on his merits. We put on the breastplate of his righteousness. We come on the basis of what he has done and not what we do. And what is the result of that? Our hearts are at peace! Paul says, "Since we are justified by faith, we have peace with God through our Lord Jesus Christ" (Romans 5:1). Calmness, courage! To use a modern term, and I think the most accurate, we have good "morale." Our morale is high. We are ready for anything. 'No ground can be too rough for Christ . . . and we have Christ. Therefore we have good morale.

In the dark days in England during the blitz, with

bombs raining down all the time, the situation was truly desperate. Then Winston Churchill would come on the radio and speak to the English people when their hearts were filled with defeat and discouragement. At times they would be almost ready to quit. But that one man's voice would ring out and the nation would take heart again—their morale would be strong. That is what Christ does. He is able to speak peace to our hearts.

You see, it is not a battle against people at all, is it? It is an inner fight, a battle in the realm of the thought life and attitudes. It is a battle in the realm of your outlook upon the situation in which you find yourself. This is the place to start. Gird up your loins with truth. Remember that in Jesus Christ you have a demonstration which no man can equal anywhere in the world. Here is the key to life, the one who is worth listening to. Believe him, Christian people, believe him! If you are Christians at all, if you have accepted Christ as the one who has the explanation for life, then believe what he says. Act on it. That is the girdle of truth.

The breastplate of righteousness protects the emotions. You do not need to be discouraged. Of course you have failed—I fail, we all fail. The One who has come understands all this. He knows we are going to fail, and he knows we are going to struggle. He knows it will be an up-and-down experience and a time of battles—and we will lose some of them. But he says, "I have taken care of all that. You do not have to stand on your merits. You stand on mine. Do not be discouraged, do not be defeated, we will win! I know what I am doing, I know how to lead you, I know what circumstances to bring you into, and I will bring you through."

The third requisite is to have the feet shod with the

preparation—the readiness—of a sense of peace. And the place to start is to remember who you are, what you are, and above all else, whom you have. Be strong in *his* strength and for *his* sake. Remember you belong to Christ's family. The Scripture says he is not ashamed to call us brothers. God is not ashamed to be called our God. Be strong for his sake. Let us get away from this subjectiveness all the time—"What is going to happen to me, and how do I feel?"—remembering that God has vested his honor in us. And remember, by putting on these three pieces of armor the battle is almost won. You will have very little difficulty overcoming evil if you start right there.

Our Father, make these words clear, plain, practical, and helpful to us. May they meet us right where we are and help us right in the conflict in which we are engaged. May our hearts be lifted up by the consciousness that the one who is in us is adequate for all things. In Christ's name, amen.

. . . besides all these, taking the shield of faith, with which you can quench all the flaming darts of the evil one (Ephesians 6:16).

6
RESISTING
THE DEVIL

There is nothing which more surely indicates we have already succumbed to the wiles of the devil than to complain about what happens to us. The Word of God invariably points out that the mark of a Christian who has learned how to *be* a Christian is that he rejoices in everything, gives thanks in all things. Now, that does not mean he enjoys everything. Nor does it mean that he merely pretends to rejoice in everything. There is nothing as ghastly as the forced smile people put on and the flippant attitude they assume in the midst of difficulties because they think this is what a Christian ought to do. It is possible to genuinely rejoice through tears, and there is nothing which more surely indicates that we have failed to understand what it means to be a Christian than a whining, complaining, griping, grousing attitude toward what happens to us in life.

Do not be surprised at the devil's attack. Of course he attacks; that is his character. That is his nature. We need not be surprised when he does this. Furthermore, God allows him to do it. This is the clear revelation of Scripture. He permits these attacks because for one thing we need them. We never would develop or grow properly if we were not attacked in this manner.

Again, it is this which ultimately accomplishes God's will. The whole outworking of God's scheme could never be brought to pass were it not that God permits the devil to do his work today within the limits of God's overriding will. Let us never forget that. God allows these things to happen, and all the writers of Scripture agree on this. Peter says, "Do not be surprised at the fiery ordeal which comes upon you to prove you, as though something strange were happening to you" (1 Peter 4:12). The Lord Jesus himself said, "In the world you have tribulation." But he adds, "Be of good cheer, I have overcome the world" (John 16:33).

But this is exactly the opposite of the way we frequently feel. We love to think that something most unusual is happening to us. No one has ever gone through what we are going through. No one has had to undergo the depression of spirit that we feel. But Paul says, "No temptation has overtaken you that is not common to man. God is faithful . . ." (1 Corinthians 10:13). So stop complaining about what happens. It is God's will for you. Let us face that. And instead of a fretful, peevish, whining attitude, let us do what the Word of God says to do when these things occur. What is that? "Put on the whole armor of God, that you may be able to stand against the wiles of the devil." There is no other way to handle it, there is no other solution to these basic human problems.

Remember, though, do not try to start with peace. When you get troubled or upset, when attacks come, do not try to start with making your heart feel at peace. This is a mistake many people make. They try to conjure up some kind of feeling of peace within and succeed only in upsetting themselves more. Do not start with peace. Start with truth. Work your way back down through truth and righteousness and you will come out at peace. This is the way to begin.

Now let us take a closer look at this battle. If we remind ourselves of these great truths, they ought to set our hearts at rest. But we all know that even though these truths often *will* set our hearts at rest, there are times when they do not. We are still depressed and filled with doubts.

Perhaps there is no good reason for us to feel this way. We may wake up in a blue mood even though we were happy when we went to bed the night before. There may be no good reason for our depression. There is nothing wrong physically (the physical elements of our lives can have a very great bearing on our feelings), but still we feel depressed.

Well, what is happening? We are experiencing what Paul calls here "the flaming darts of the evil one." These stratagems of Satan come to us in various forms. Sometimes they are evil thoughts and imaginations which intrude suddenly upon our thinking, often at the most incongruous times. We may be reading the Bible; we may be bowed in prayer; we may be thinking about something else entirely when all of a sudden some filthy, lewd thought flashes into our mind. What is this? One of the fiery darts of the evil one! We ought to recognize it as such.

Sometimes these darts come as doubts and even blasphemies—sudden feelings that perhaps this business of Christianity is nothing after all but a big hoax or a dream. Perhaps we feel that it can all be explained psychologically or that Jesus Christ was a victim of self-delusion. Perhaps the world is not the way we have been taught to believe it is, and things are not the way the Bible says. You have doubtless experienced these times of doubt. All Christians have had this sudden feeling that perhaps it is all a fantasy. Again, these fiery darts may come in the form of sudden fears, anxieties, fleeting sensations that things are all wrong. We cannot seem to shake them off.

The Devil's Whispers

These feelings, in whatever form they may take, are always from the same source. They are the fiery darts of the wicked one. We are the biggest fools on earth if we do not see them in that light and deal with them as such. And in whatever form they may come to us, they always have two characteristics. First, they seem to arise out of our own thoughts. They seem to come right from our inner selves. We feel, "This is something I am thinking," and oftentimes it is a shocking thing.

But the devil is really whispering to us. He is influencing us. Ah yes, but it doesn't seem like that to us. In our ignorance and innocence we blame ourselves. "How can I think a thing like this if I am a Christian? Can a Christian have such a lewd and filthy thought as this? Can I really be a Christian if I think like this? I must not be one after all."

This, of course, is exactly why the devil sent those thoughts to you. He wants you to think that way. If it is doubt (and we are always exposed to doubts, these sudden attacks upon faith, these sudden feelings that Christianity is not as sure and certain as it once seemed to us), we say to ourselves, "I must have already lost my faith or I would not think like this. What is the matter with me? How can I be a Christian and even have such a thought?" So we try to repress the thought. We think, "There must be something wrong; we should not feel like this," and we push the thought down into our subconscious. But it is still there, lurking underneath, and we feel dishonest because we are not even willing to look at it and face it. This takes its toll on us in physical ways as well as in mental and emotional strain and tension.

We feel uncertain and confused because we are convinced that the opposite of faith is doubt. We think if we have doubts we cannot have faith and if we have faith we do not have doubts. Therefore, if we have doubts, we cannot be men and women of faith. We fail to recognize this as the lie of the devil.

The second characteristic is that doubts are always an attack upon our position in Christ as the truth—as our righteousness and our peace. These darts are always an insinuation of doubt about those matters—never about anything else. They are an attack upon those areas of faith.

This is always the way of the devil. He said to Eve in the garden, "Has God said unto thee . . . did God say that . . . ?" There is the implication of doubt. He said to Jesus in the temptation in the wilderness, "*If* thou be the Son of God, then turn these stones into bread." IF! There is the insinuation that these things are not true. This is the way he raises doubts, creates guilt, arouses fear. These are the attacks of the evil one.

The Quenching Process

Now, what are we to do? How are we to combat these attacks successfully? Well, the apostle says, "Take the shield of faith, with which you can quench all the flaming darts of the evil one." Notice that he did not say the "shield of belief." We have already reminded ourselves of our belief when we have put on the girdle of truth, our breastplate of righteousness, and the equipment of the gospel of peace. That is our belief in what Christ is to us.

But faith is more than that. This is very important to see. Faith is acting upon belief. Faith is decision, action, resolution. Faith is saying, "Yes, I believe Christ is the truth. He is my righteousness, he is my peace. *Therefore* this, and this, and this, must follow." Faith is working out the implications of belief. When you say *therefore,* you move from belief into faith. Faith is particularizing; it is taking the general truth and applying it to the specific situation and saying, "If this be truth, then this must follow." That is the shield of faith.

Now, have you learned how to take the shield of faith when doubts come? Do you say, "Christ is the truth. He is the basic revelation of things which really are. He has demonstrated it. *Therefore,* I cannot accept the thought that Christianity is a hoax. I cannot believe that Christ is the truth and that my doubts are true, too. I have committed myself to Christ because I have been persuaded that he has demonstrated truth fully. I stand on that ground. *Therefore* I must reject this insinuation."

Do you reason that "Christ is the truth, *therefore* I cannot believe this subtle philosophy which exalts man and makes God unnecessary in human affairs. I must reject it. Since I have found Christ true, I cannot believe this sudden feeling I have of unreality. I must regard it as what Christ says it is: from the devil. Jesus Christ says he is a liar from the beginning. Therefore this is a lie and I reject it."

Is this the way you think it through? Our problem is that we have become so accustomed to believing our feelings as though they were facts. We never examine them. We never take them and look at them and ask, "Is this true?" We simply say, "I feel this way. Therefore it must be true." This is why so many are constantly defeated; they accept their feelings as facts. Rather, we are to say, "Christ is my righteousness. I am linked with him. I am one with him. His life is my life and my life is his life. We are married. *Therefore* I cannot believe this lie that these evil thoughts are my thoughts. They are not my thoughts at all. They are thoughts which come because of another force. It is not my thinking at all. No, it is the devil again. I do not want these thoughts. I do not like them. I reject them. I do not want them in my thinking; therefore they are not mine. They are the devil's children, and I'll spank them and send them back where they belong!"

Using the shield of faith means refusal to feel condemned or to feel guilty. "God loves me. He says so. He says nothing will change that. Nothing will separate us. Nothing I do or fail to do will separate us! All right, then I will believe that, and I will not believe the thought that God does not love me and want me." You see, you cannot entertain both thoughts. "No man can serve two masters."

Christ is the ground of my peace. Therefore it is his responsibility to take me through every situation. So I cannot, I will not believe this fear, this sudden anxiety which grips my heart. I will not believe that it is from me. It is simply sent to shake my confidence

in Christ. It is an attempt to destroy my peace. But
Christ is adequate for even this, and I refuse to
change.

Proof of Faith's Reality

This is what James calls "resisting the devil." This
is the shield of faith. It is refusing to believe the lie
that if you have doubts you cannot have faith. Because that *is* a lie. Doubt is always an attack on faith.
The fact that you have doubt *proves* that you have
faith. They are not opposites at all. Doubt is the proof
of the reality of faith. Therefore reexamine the ground
of your faith and reassert it. Remember that feelings
are not necessarily facts at all.

And James says further that if you keep on resisting the devil he will flee from you (James 4:7). Think
of that! He will flee from you. Resist the devil again
and again every time an evil thought or doubt comes
back. Refuse to give up your position. And sooner or
later, inevitably the doubts will clear, your feelings
will change, the attacks cease, and you will be back
again in the sunshine of faith and the experience of
the love and joy of God.

That is what Paul is talking about when he says,
"Take the shield of faith. It is able to quench every
fiery dart of the evil one." The shield of faith is
enough in itself. It is all you need. You do not really
need the other two pieces of armor. It may sound
strange to say that, but it is true. You do not need any
more because the shield of faith is able to quench
every fiery dart of the wicked one. It alone would see
you through, if that were all you had.

Then why are we given more? Because we are not
only to be conquerors. The Bible says we are to be
"more than conquerors" (Romans 8:37). We are not
only to win; we are to win victoriously, triumphantly,
abundantly. Remember that John said, "He who is

in you is greater than he who is in the world" (1 John 4:4). Paul adds, "Where sin increased, grace abounded all the more" (Romans 5:20). We are intended to do more than barely make it to heaven. We are designed to triumph, to be fearless, to be not only unconquered but unconquerable!

I think so often of these words of Rudyard Kipling, describing the pressures of life:

> *If you can keep your head when all about you*
> *Are losing theirs and blaming it on you;*
> *If you can trust yourself when all men doubt you,*
> *But make allowance for their doubting too;*
> *If you can wait and not be tired by waiting,*
> *Or, being lied about, don't deal in lies,*
> *Or, being hated, don't give away to hating,*
> *And yet don't look too good, nor talk too wise;*
>
> *If you can dream—and not make dreams your*
>   *master;*
> *If you can think—and not make thoughts your*
>   *aim;*
> *If you can meet with Triumph and Disaster*
> *And treat those two imposters just the same;*
> *If you can bear to hear the truth you've spoken*
> *Twisted by knaves to make a trap for fools,*
> *Or watch the things you gave your life to broken,*
> *And stoop and build 'em up with worn out tools;*
>
> *If you can talk with crowds and keep your virtue,*
> *Or walk with kings—nor lose the common*
>   *touch;*
> *If neither foes nor loving friends can hurt you;*
> *If all men count with you, but none too much;*
> *If you can fill the unforgiving minute*
> *With sixty seconds' worth of distance run—*
> *Yours is the earth and everything that's in it,*
> *And—which is more—you'll be a Man, my*
>   *son!*

That is a very eloquent description of life. It is exactly what the Word of God is designed to prepare us for. That is what it means to be "strong in the Lord and in the strength of his might."

Our Father, help us to be men and women of faith, to realize that your word has brought to us the truth as it is in Jesus. Let us not fling away our confidence nor cast away our reliance upon that unshakable word, but trust in you and show to the world that this is the only thing which can keep a man or a woman standing in the midst of pressures which defeat and ruin and blast and destroy life. We pray in Christ's name, amen.

And take the helmet of salvation, and the sword of the Spirit, which is the word of God (Ephesians 6:17).

7
HOPE FOR
CLEAR HEADS

The shield of faith alone would enable us to overcome anything life might hand us and to extinguish all of Satan's flaming missiles of doubt and confusion, disillusionment and fear. However, God has given us still more defensive equipment so we may become "more than conquerors." We are expected to give intelligent consideration to the process of overcoming and to learning how to counteract the attacks of Satan in our lives. It is the whole armor of God which makes this possible.

I Am in Christ

Before going on to a consideration of the remaining pieces of armor, I would like to suggest another perspective to increase our understanding of the significance of this armor of God. We have seen that it is a figurative explanation of Jesus Christ and what he is to us. But also the armor is an expansion of Jesus' words, "You in me, and I in you" (John 14:20). That is the defense of the Christian. "You in me, and I in you." Those are some of the simplest words in the English language. Any child can understand them. They are monosyllables, yet they encompass a truth so profound that I wonder if anyone can ever remotely apprehend all that is involved in these simple words.

The first three pieces of this armor that Paul describes— girding your loins with the girdle of truth, putting on the breastplate of righteousness, and having your feet shod with the equipment of the gospel of peace—are a figurative way of explaining or expounding the phrase, "You in me," or the "Christian in Christ." When we came to Jesus Christ and believed in him, we were "in Christ"; we had a different basis of living and found Christ to be the ground of truth, the key to life.

Then we discovered that we are invited by God to rest upon Christ's righteousness. In the amazing experience of the cross, God has transferred our sin to Christ and transferred his righteousness to us. This is the ground of our acceptance before God and the answer to the problem of human guilt from which we all suffer. It was then we learned that Christ is our peace, the source of our sense of calm and well-being.

He Is in Me

Now the last three pieces of armor describe what it means for Christ to be in the Christian—Christ appropriated, applied to actual life. These last three pieces are very practical and highly important to us. We have already seen what it means to take "the shield of faith, with which you can quench all the flaming darts of the evil one." The reason we so often experience weakness is that we do not actually take it. We continually try to muddle through. We do not do intelligently what God says and apply the shield of faith, thus drawing practical conclusions from the ground of faith we have taken.

There are only two pieces of the armor left—the helmet of salvation and the sword of the Spirit. Now we must examine what is meant by this phrase, "the helmet of salvation." The figure of a helmet immediately suggests to us that this is something designed to protect the mind, the intelligence, the ability to think and reason.

Earlier we saw that the breastplate was the protection of our emotional life. When you figuratively put on Christ as your breastplate of righteousness, you are assuming a position in him which protects you from the sense of guilt and unforgiveness—the most common ground of disturbance to the emotions. It is because we feel guilty that we get emotionally upset and depressed, and the breastplate protects us there. The shoes, as we have already seen, protect us in the area of our will. The shoes of the gospel of peace (Christ is our peace) create a readiness and willingness within us. It is our motivations which are dealt with here. Christ as our peace motivates us and makes us ready to face life.

But the helmet is designed for the head, for the intelligence, the mind. If we follow through consistently in our application of these pieces of armor, we will discover that the helmet represents something Christ is doing in us and through us in the world.

This helmet can keep our thinking straight and preserve us from mental confusion and darkness.

Confessions of Confusion

Stop a minute here. I would like to ask you this: As you look at our world, is there anything more desperately needed or more relevant to the situation in which we find ourselves than something to keep us thinking straight? Was there ever a time when men were more frankly bewildered than they are in our day or when statesmen are more openly confused and honestly admit it? The intelligentsia confess to being utterly baffled in dealing with the problems with which human society is confronted.

Just think about the staggering complexity of the issues of our day—birth control, race relations, crime and delinquency, moral decay, disarmament, and the teeming misery of our vast city slums. The mind is simply overwhelmed by the insolubility of the problems which face human lives. No wonder H. G. Wells wrote at the close of World War II:

> *Quite apart from any bodily depression, the spectacle of evil in the world—the wanton destruction of homes, the ruthless hounding of decent folk into exile, the bombings of open cities, the cold-blooded massacres and mutilations of children and defenseless gentle folk, the rapes and filthy humiliations, and above all, the return of deliberate and organized torture, mental torment and fear, to a world from which such things had seemed well-nigh banished—all these have come near to breaking my spirit altogether.*

Listen to this startling statement by George Bernard Shaw:

*The science to which I pinned my faith is bankrupt.
Its counsels, which should have established the mil-
lennium, led instead directly to the suicide of
Europe. I believed them once. In their name I helped
to destroy the faith of millions of worshippers in the
temples of a thousand creeds. And now they look at
me and witness the great tragedy of an atheist who
has lost his faith.*

What a revealing confession of mental confusion and
darkness by some of the great leaders of thought in
our day! There is no protection in the world for the
mind.

A Future Salvation

But the Christian has the helmet of salvation.
"Well," you say, "what is that? What is the helmet,
this protection, which keeps our thinking straight in
the midst of a very confused world?" Paul answers in
one word—it is the helmet of *salvation*. He is not talking about the salvation of the soul. He is not referring
to salvation as regeneration or conversion. In other
words, he is not looking back at all. He is not speaking of salvation as a past decision which was once
made, or even as a present experience, but he is looking on to the future. He is talking about a salvation
which will be a future event. It is exactly what he is
referring to in Romans when he says, "Salvation is
nearer to us now than when we first believed" (Romans 13:11).

This helmet is further defined for us by the apostle
in his first letter to the Thessalonians: "But, since we
belong to the day [we who are Christians], let us be
sober, and put on the breastplate of faith and love,
and for a helmet the hope of salvation" (1 Thessalonians 5:8). Here salvation is a hope, something yet in

the future, something as yet not possessed or entered
into fully. This future tense of salvation is described
for us in a number of passages, but it is discussed very
plainly and fully in Romans:

> *We know that the whole creation has been groaning
> in travail together until now; and not only the
> creation, but we ourselves, who have the first fruits
> of the Spirit, groan inwardly as we wait for adop-
> tion as sons, the redemption of our bodies. For in
> this hope we were saved. Now hope that is seen is
> not hope. For who hopes for what he sees? But if we
> hope for what we do not see, we wait for it with
> patience (Romans 8:22-25).*

What is Paul talking about? About the day of resurrection, the day of the coming again of Christ, the
day when creation will be delivered from its bondage
by Christ's return to establish his kingdom. This helmet, therefore, is the recognition that all human
schemes to obtain world peace and harmony are
doomed to fail. But *through these failures,* Jesus Christ
is working out his own plan which will culminate in
his appearing again and in the establishment of his
own reign in righteousness on the earth. That is the
helmet of salvation which will keep your thinking
straight in the hour of man's utter confusion and
darkness.

The principle of God's working is declared over
and over again in Scripture. It is written for all to
read. "No flesh," God says, "shall glory in my presence." In other words, nothing that man can boast of
shall contribute one iota to the final solution of the
human dilemma. It is all of God. He will establish
it, and not all of human wisdom, not all our vaunted
knowledge and scientific discoveries will contribute
one thing to the ultimate solution. According to the

record of Scripture, all that man boasts in shall crumble into dust, and those things which can be shaken shall be shaken, and only those which cannot be shaken shall remain. Those are the things of God. No flesh shall glory in his presence.

But that isn't the whole idea. Do not stop there. If you do, you will be guilty of the extremism by which the devil keeps us off balance and eccentric in our thinking. God is working through these events of history, but he is working out his purposes on a basis totally different from the aims and goals of men. That is the helmet of salvation. Therefore Christians are not to be taken in by the unreal and groundless expectations of the world, nor are they to withdraw from these and isolate themselves.

Christians are to be involved in what is going on in the world for wholly different reasons than the worldling has. Christians are to be involved in order to accomplish God's desire to confront men everywhere, at every level, in all enterprises of life, with the good news of God's salvation in Jesus Christ. Is that clear? If we see that, it will save much heartache, delusion, disappointment, and confusion as you read your daily newspaper.

Why is it that thoughtful minds such as those of H. G. Wells and George Bernard Shaw are so bewildered by what they find in life? It is because they pinned their hopes on wholly unstable, unrealistic resources. As the Dean of Melbourne wrote concerning H. G. Wells:

> *He hailed science as a panacea for all ills and the goddess of knowledge and power. In a series of popular scientific romances he visualized the luminous* Shape of Things to Come. *In* Foods of the Gods *he described a future of bigger and better*

men. He spoke of a planned world, of eugenics, of
mechanized labor, of scientific diet and scientific
education.

How much we still hear these phrases tossed about in
our own day! But all of this fails. These thinkers built
their grandiose dreams on a cloud, a cobweb, a shifting, shimmering illusion. And when the illusion
changed shape, as all illusions eventually must, then
their castles in the clouds came tumbling down. That
has been the repeated pattern of history for twenty or
more centuries—men building upon shifting,
ephemeral, and temporary things instead of on the
unshakable things which always remain, to which
the Scriptures give testimony.

But the Christian has a helmet of salvation. He has
a hope for the future. He has an understanding that
God is working out his purpose, and therefore he is
not disturbed when human programs go wrong and
everything fails—when the New Deal and the Fair
Deal and the Great Society and all the other fancy
names for human progress end up in the same old
place, time after time after time. The Christian has
learned to *expect* wars and rumors of wars unto the
very end. He *expects* false teachings and false philosophies and cults and heresies to abound. He is told all
this will happen. It is part of the program, part of the
total overall plan and purpose and moving of God in
history.

The Christian knows that wars are unavoidable,
even though every effort should be made to avoid
them, and that there is no contradiction in this. The
Christian knows that war is madness and that nothing is really solved by war. But he knows also that we
are living in a mad world, a world that is deluded by
silken, subtle, satanic lies which are deliberately de-

signed to end up in the mangling and mutilating of the bodies and souls of men.

The world is in such a state and condition that the Christian knows the innocent and the weak will suffer and nothing much can be done about it at times. The blame lies squarely on the stubborn refusal of men everywhere to believe the true nature of the problem and the remedy that God's love has fully provided. The Christian knows that demonic forces can rise and possess the world from time to time—and will do so—and every human scheme to control them will ultimately fail.

Well then, what shall we do? Shall we withdraw from life? Shall we give ourselves to building our own little airtight capsule of life and look forward to retirement? Shall we rise up and fight the United Nations or let the world go to hell? God forgive us, this too often has been the answer of Christians these days.

The helmet of the hope of salvation not only tells us that these things are happening and will happen, but that a certain, sure salvation is coming, *and it is even now at work.* This is what we need to know. Not merely that it will finally end right, but that the ending is being worked out now! History is not a meaningless jumble but a controlled pattern, and the Lord Jesus Christ is the One who is directing these events. He is the Lord of history. God is at work in the self-same events that we look at with such horror and confusion.

We cannot identify ourselves with all the methods of the worldlings or even with all their aims, but we can identify ourselves with their persons. We do not need to join their causes, but we need to listen to them and to show ourselves concerned about them as people. We can be their friend without joining causes, and if they balk at that, the choice is theirs and not ours. Jesus said, " 'A servant is not greater than his master.' If they persecuted me, they will persecute you; if they kept my word, they will keep yours also" (John 15:20). We can expect both reactions as we try to involve ourselves in life around us, not in order to advance these hopeless causes, but to interest and concern ourselves with the people involved.

There are also many causes that the Christian *can* join. There are aims which he can wholeheartedly endorse. Christians are always to be humanitarian—helping the weak, ministering to the sick, helping those who are old and in prison or burdened in any way. The Christian should always be ready to further good government, because government is of God. Even the worst of governments has a basic commitment and relationship to God. "The powers that be are ordained of God," the Scripture says.

Therefore the Christian ought to be ready to alleviate social evil and to further understanding between countries if he can. Read the injunctions of Scripture: "Honor all men." "Do good to all." "Honor the king." "Obey your masters." "Provide things honest before all men." "Feed the hungry, clothe the naked, heal the sick." These are practical exhortations, are they not?

Look at the life of the Lord Jesus himself. Many are asking today, "Would Jesus have joined a nuclear freeze committee if he had been here?" or "Would he have marched to Washington D.C. in defense of 'human rights'?" The answer is perfectly predictable. He would not have joined any committee, just as he joined no social movement in his own day—and there were plenty of them existing then. But he would have been the friend to any who sincerely, even though mistakenly, were seeking to do good.

Jesus would have been the angry, vocal foe of any who were hypocritically using a cause to advance their own purposes or to dirty and defile the minds and hearts of others. As he stood before Pilate, Jesus said, "My kingship is not of this world" (John 18:36). That is, "I am no threat to you, Pilate. My kingdom is not of this world. I am not involved in any political maneuverings that you think might be a threat to your position." Nevertheless he was known everywhere as the Friend of sinners.

Hope Laid Aside

All this is possible to us only if we put on as a helmet the hope of salvation. One of the great reasons the church is so confused in this day and is saying so little of true significance to the world is that it has laid aside, by and large, the hope of the coming of the Lord. There are very few sermons preached on it; very little is said about it. There is no time given to a consideration of what it means and why it is set forth so frequently and so clearly in the Scriptures. Great sections of the Scriptures that deal with this event are simply ignored among Christians. As a result, our thinking is muddled and confused. The church does not know which side to take or where to stand. It has nothing to say. Or at best it gives an uncertain sound which calls no one to battle and encourages no heart.

We are to remind ourselves frequently of the coming of the Lord. How many times did he say, "Watch! Watch therefore, that you may be ready for that hour." We must live daily in its hope and anticipation. The battle is not ours. This is not merely a private fight we are engaged in. We have been talking about this great struggle against the devil and his angels, against the principalities and powers, against the wiles of the devil, as though it were primarily a private fight. It does come down to that at last. It meets us right where we live—in our homes, our offices, our relationship with our fellow human beings. But it is not only that, it is always good to remember that the battle is not ours, but the Lord's. We are individual units fighting in a great army. The ultimate cause is sure and the end is certain. We do not need to be troubled by all the things happening on the face of the earth, for our Conqueror has already won.

Though we may be hard pressed in our immediate realm in this battle, the cause is never in doubt. The end is absolutely certain; the outcome is sure; the battle is the Lord's. It is not finally and ultimately a struggle between us and the devil but a struggle between Christ and Satan. God is always at work in human life and in society. He is at work through his body to heal and to help, to love and to suffer, until that morning without clouds shall dawn and the day break and every shadow flee away.

Are you frightened by world prospects? Well, let me tell you this: It is going to get much worse! Jesus said men's hearts shall fail them for fear because of things that are coming to pass on the face of the earth. If you think it is hard to stand now, if these things throw you for a loss now, what will it be when the darkness increases, the cause looks hopeless, and things get very much worse? That is the hour when we must have the hope of salvation—the helmet to protect the mind. The writer of Hebrews says, "We do not yet see everything in subjection to him [man]. But we see Jesus" (Hebrews 2:8-9). It is that which sustains the mind in all hours of pressure.

Here in this favored land of ours we have so much for which we can give thanks. God in grace has granted that we might be relatively free from so much that bothers and distresses others. But there are great areas of the world already where faith is not permitted to be expressed openly, where the darkness is far greater than here, where the forces of wrong seem to be striding in unopposed triumph through the land, and nothing seems to stand in their way. What do Christians do in those places? There is only one thing they can do—they must put on the helmet of the hope of salvation. This will keep their thinking straight. It directs them in the causes to which they give themselves. It gives them advice and counsel as to where they should put their efforts and in what they should make investments of time and money and enterprise.

It can do the same for us. We need not succumb to the delusion of the world—that redemption, salvation, and the working out of all human problems by the application of human intelligence is just beyond the horizon where everything will be all right. How long has the world grasped at that futile dream? Read the writings of the ancient Greek philosophers and you will see that they were saying the same things then. And as far back as human history goes, men have ever been grasping after this illusive hope that something can be worked out here.

But God has never said that. Consistently throughout the Scripture, he has said that man in his fallen condition is unable—absolutely and totally unable—to work out his problems. But in the strength of the hope of salvation we can keep our minds and our hearts calm and undisturbed in the day of battle, in the day of darkness.

Father, thank you for this reassuring word. We know that things are not nearly as bad as they could be, or even perhaps as they will be. But we thank you for the constant assurance you give to us that even when they get worse they are in your control, that nothing can come which you do not permit, nothing can happen which is not already anticipated and worked out, that the battle is the Lord's. Thank you for the certainty that we stand in the power of God and in the strength of his might, and that our hope is not in the flimsy constructions of men but in the eternal purposes of a living God. Thank you for this encouragement to our hearts. In Christ's name, amen.

And take the helmet of salvation, and the sword of the Spirit, which is the word of God (Ephesians 6:17).

8
SWORDSMANSHIP

Now we come to the last of these pieces of the Christian's armor, "the sword of the Spirit, which is the word of God." The first thing we must say is that this, again, is Christ. Christ is our life, if we are Christians at all, but this is Christ made practically available to us through the sayings of his word. I think it is very important to stress this. It is so easy to be Christians in general but not in specific. It is so very easy to have a vague sense of following Christ but not know exactly, in specific terms, what this means. But that is why the Word of God has been given to us; Christian truth as a whole is more than we can handle—it is the individual promises that make Christianity manageable.

In writing to the Colossians the apostle Paul says,

> *Let the word of Christ dwell in you richly, {as you} teach and admonish one another in all wisdom, and {as you} sing psalms and hymns and spiritual songs with thankfulness in your hearts to God (Colossians 3:16).*

By that he is indicating that the authority of Jesus Christ and the authority of the Scripture is one and the same thing. There are many today who challenge that. There are many voices that tell us that as Christians we must follow Christ and accept the authority of Christ, but we need not accept the authority of the Bible. But Paul answers that by calling the Scriptures "the word of Christ." You cannot separate the two.

I once attended a meeting of ministers at which we listened to a professor who is a Christian read a very excellent and helpful paper on science and the Christian faith. After he had finished, certain questions were addressed to him by members of the group. One man said, "Sir, I can accept the Bible as a witness of certain men to what they thought of Jesus Christ. But you seem to go further. You have used the word *inspired* on several occasions in your paper and that seems to suggest that in your opinion the Bible is more than the views of men, that it has divine authority. Is this true?"

The Christian professor gave a very wise answer: "My answer may sound to you very much like Sunday school propaganda, but I can only put it this way: The center of my life is Jesus Christ. I have found him to be the key to everything that I desire in life. And yet I could know nothing about Christ if I did not learn it from the Bible. The Bible presents Christ and

Christ defines the Bible. How can I make a distinction between the two?" With considerable embarrassment the questioner threw up his hands and changed the subject.

The authority of Scripture *is* the authority of Jesus Christ; they are indivisible. To attempt to distinguish the two is like asking which blade of a pair of scissors is more important or which leg of a pair of pants is more necessary. We know Christ through the Bible, and we understand the Bible through the knowledge of Christ—the two cannot be separated. That is why Paul calls it "the word of Christ."

The Sayings of God

Now in the verse we are looking at—"The sword of the Spirit, which is the word of God"—it is important to see that it is not the complete Bible that is referred to by the phrase "the word of God." There are two words that are used in Scripture for *the Word*. There is the familiar word *logos,* which is used in the opening verse of John's gospel, "In the beginning was the Word [Logos], and the Logos was with God, and the Logos was God." Then there is another word, used less frequently, *hrema,* which is somewhat different in meaning than the first.

The word *logos* refers to the total utterance of God, the complete revelation of what God has said. The second word means a specific saying of God, a passage or a verse which has special application to an immediate situation. It implies an existential use of the Word of God; that is, applied to experience, to our existence.

The second word is the one used here. The "sword of the Spirit" is the saying of God applied to a specific situation. That is the great weapon placed in the hands of the believer. Perhaps you have had some

experience with this. Sometimes when you are reading a passage of Scripture, the words seem suddenly
to come alive, take on flesh and bones, and leap off
the page at you, or grow eyes that follow you around
everywhere you go, or develop a voice that echoes in
your ears until you cannot get away from it. Perhaps
you have had that experience in some moment of
temptation or doubt when you were assailed by what
Paul calls here "the flaming darts of the evil one."
And immediately a passage of Scripture which
supplies the answer comes flashing to mind.

Or perhaps you have been asked a question that
caught you off guard for a moment and you were
about to say, "I don't know," when suddenly you had
a moment of illumination and a word of Scripture
came to mind which gave the answer. Perhaps this experience has happened while you were sitting in a
meeting where some message has come home to your
heart with strange and powerful effect. You were
greatly moved, and in that moment you made a deep
and permanent decision.

All this is the *hrema* of God, the sayings of God
that strike home like arrows to the heart. This is
called the sword *of the Spirit* because it is not only
originated by him as the author of the Word but it is
also recalled to mind by the Spirit and made powerful
by him in our lives. It is his answer to the attack of
the devil who comes to discourage us; the Spirit
brings a word to our mind to parry the thrust of the
devil.

The Only Offense

Now, as a sword the Word is useful both for defense
and for offense. This, by the way, is the only part of
the armor that can be used for offense. It both defends
and protects us, but it also pierces other hearts and

destroys the lies of the devil in others besides our-selves. That is its great effect.

The Word is the only proper offense that the Christian has. He is to proclaim the truth. He does not need to defend it; he does not need to support it with long and extensive arguments. There is a place for that, but not in an encounter with those who disbelieve. He is to proclaim it, simply to declare it. As the Scripture says in Hebrews: "For the word of God is living and active, sharper than any two-edged sword, piercing to the division of soul and spirit, of joints and marrow, and discerning the thoughts and intentions of the heart" (Hebrews 4:12). It gets below the reason and pierces the armor that has been erected against it and comes home to the heart. Thus it has power in itself.

Now, it is this offensive quality which explains why the Bible is so continuously under attack. For centuries the enemies of the gospel, prompted by the devil, have been seeking to destroy the Bible. This effort has been directed both toward the very existence of the Bible and seeking to destroy its significance. In our day, though, the attack is primarily directed toward a destruction of its significance. With very clever words and subtle arguments the devil speaks through men of prominence and intelligence to destroy the testimony of the Scriptures.

This does not mean that the men themselves are necessarily hypocritical. It is not that they are being deliberately and knowingly destructive. Many of them are sincerely attempting to be what they may describe as "honest to God." But notice the focus of these intelligent and subtle arguments: They are always an attempt to disprove the historicity of the biblical record, particularly in relation to supernatural events. These men cannot accept the idea that an invisible realm, which the Bible calls the kingdom of God, has invaded our commonplace realm of space and time. Such a concept is distasteful to them, so their attacks are aimed at making the Bible accounts appear incredible and therefore unreliable. To the extent they succeed, people will no longer take the Scripture seriously.

These speakers and professors and doctors of theology claim to be theologians and Bible scholars, but they betray the Scriptures with the kiss of Judas and mislead thousands. The effect, of course, is to keep people from reading the Scriptures. That is the main thing. The devil makes this fantastic effort because he knows the power of the Scripture, and his whole aim is to keep people from seriously and thoughtfully reading the Scriptures. For of course all that is needed to answer the attacks of the scholars is simply to read these accounts in a thoughtful and serious way.

Let me illustrate that with the Christmas story. Nothing is more basic and central to the Christian message than the story of the way the infinite God became a babe in a manger and was welcomed with the angels' song, a brilliant star, the coming of the shepherds and of the wise men. We love the simple beauty of that ancient story. It transforms the world, at least outwardly, for a brief time every year and has done so for twenty centuries.

But the false prophets of our day treat this story as if it were nothing but a myth, a pretty story. There is no attempt at all to disprove the supernatural claims of the biblical story—they are merely dismissed with a wave of the hand. Scorn is heaped upon them as unworthy of modern intelligence. The implication is clear that any who believe in this story are in a class with those who still believe in a flat earth or the existence of fairies.

The reason for this, of course, is that any acceptance of this account as a historical fact means that its implications cannot be shaken aside. We must face it as an incontrovertible event that can only be explained by the explanation which Scripture gives: the need of men in their lost condition for an invasion of God to accomplish a work of redemption at great cost to himself and thus set men free.

A Simple Tale

What is the answer to the false claims that accounts of supernatural events are merely myths? Well, simply read the scriptural accounts. Read the Christmas story as told by Matthew and Luke. As you read the familiar tale, see how artlessly and simply it is presented, how uncontrived the record is. There is no attempt to garnish it or to bolster it with arguments or theological explanations. There is just the simple narrative of what happened to a couple on their way to Bethlehem, what occurred when they arrived there, and what happened in the immediate days following. When the story is set in place in the total narrative of the Bible, how fitting it is, how natural and unforced.

As G. Campbell Morgan so beautifully put it, "The song of the angels to sighing humanity is the beginning of the infinite mystery of an incarnate God. From that simple story all light is streaming, all hope is flaming, all songs are coming." Wesley captures this in his hymn,

> *Late in time behold him come,*
> *Offspring of the Virgin's womb:*
> *Veiled in flesh, the Godhead see;*
> *Hail the Incarnate Deity,*
> *Pleased as man with men to dwell,*
> *Jesus, our Emmanuel.*

Now we need only remember that this simple un-complicated story was widely accepted and proclaimed in the first century. Along with the account of the cross and the resurrection, that story has changed the world. No Christian in Scripture ever denies it. No apostle, or even Jesus himself, ever questioned these events, ever suggested that they did not take place exactly as recorded. And the stories were well known in their day.

In other words, this account reflects the inherent ability of truth, simply told, to compel belief without artificial support. As we read the account, it wins the submission of our reason, it appeals to the love of the heart, it compels the obedience of the will. To reject it, therefore, is to violate our basic humanity. This is why John declared in a letter written toward the close of the first century that this story is one of the tests of false teachers. He declared that if someone denies the incarnation and says that Jesus did not come in the flesh, he is inspired by a wrong spirit and is an antichrist (1 John 4:2-3).

The Sword in Action

The purpose of the Word, these "sayings of God," is to compel belief in the face of any distortion of truth. They are a sword of the Spirit to defend against that which would undermine and attack ultimate authority. Looking back in my own life I am aware of many times when this sword of the Spirit has saved me from error and delusion of some kind or another. As a young Christian, I was stopped at the edge of disobedience many times when some temptation seemed so logical, so reasonable, so widely practiced that I was allured by it. I was often arrested by a word that I had memorized as a young Christian and which has come to me many times since. It is in the book of

Proverbs, "Trust in the LORD with all your heart, and do not rely on your own insight" (Proverbs 3:5).

It is so easy to think that because something *looks* logical to us it must be logical. But we fail to recognize the fact that we are easily deceived. We are not the rational creatures we love to think we are. There is much illusion and delusion in our world, and we are not intelligent enough to see through this phantasma, these lies. Therefore the word comes, "Trust in the Lord with all your heart." Believe the truth as it is revealed, and "lean not to your own understanding."

Sometimes a sword of the Spirit has been placed in my hand not before defeat, but right in the midst of it or right afterward. It has thus become the means of preventing any painful recurrences. I remember when a word from James came home to me with unusual power after a very violent and nasty display of temper on my part. A verse flashed into my mind which I had read in the letter of James, "The anger of man does not work the righteousness of God" (James 1:20). That arrested me. I thought, here I am claiming to be interested in working the righteousness of God, and what am I doing? . . . losing my temper, flaring up at someone, and then thinking I am accomplishing what God sent me to do. That verse stopped me then and has been a help ever since.

I remember another time when my heart was once pierced by these words from the book of Proverbs: "Only by pride comes contention." When we get involved in contention and strife with one another, it is so easy to blame the other fellow. He started it! One day a nephew of mine and my daughter were fighting, and I asked them, "Who started it?" The boy said, "She did. She hit me back." That is so human, is it not? Ah, but the Word says, "Only by pride

comes contention." Where there is strife and contention, pride is at work and both parties are usually
guilty of it.

As a young Christian, I recall how the powerful
lure to sexual misbehavior which exists in this world
was frequently dispelled in my thinking by the sudden flashing recollection of that word in Ephesians
where the apostle says, "Let no one deceive you with
empty words [and that is exactly what they try to do],
for it is because of these things [the context is that of
sexual wrong] that the wrath of God comes upon the
sons of disobedience" (Ephesians 5:6). That arrested
me when I first heard it. Later, when I came to understand more fully what the wrath of God means—that
it is not a lightning bolt from heaven or an auto acci-
dent or something like that, but rather it is the certain disintegration of life, the dehumanizing, the
brutalization of life that comes when one gives way
to these kinds of things—it took on even more power
in my life.

Several years ago there was a man who came to
counsel with me every week for over a year who was in
the grip of a terrible depression of spirit, an utter de-
solation of mind. I have never met such a lonely, miserable man. He shut himself away from everyone. His
liberation began by repeatedly praying one single
phrase of Scripture. It was all the Scripture he could
in faith lay hold of. He rejected everything else I tried
to point out to him. But one phrase stuck with him,
and he prayed it again and again: "Not my will but
thine be done." At last, slowly, like the sun coming
up, the light began to dawn, and you could see the
change in his life. Today he is living a normal, free
life, set free by "the sword of the Spirit which is the
saying of God."

Obviously, the greater exposure there is to Scripture the more the Spirit can use this mighty sword in our lives. If you never read or study your Bible, you are terribly exposed to defeat and despair. You have no defense; you have nothing to put up against these forces that are at work. Therefore, learn to read your Bible regularly. Read all of Scripture, for each section has a special purpose.

The Christian who neglects the reading of the Scripture is in direct disobedience to the will of the Lord. The Lord Jesus said, "It is they [the Scriptures] that bear witness to me" (John 5:39). That is the way you come to know Christ. There is no way apart from the Scriptures. And there is no way to come into full maturity as a Christian apart from the Scripture.

Now, finally, what is the responsibility of the Christian when the Spirit places one of these sayings in your mind on some appropriate occasion as a sword? What are you to do? Well, the apostle says, take it! Heed it! Obey it! Do not reject it or treat it lightly. Take it seriously. The Spirit of God has brought it to mind for a purpose; therefore give heed to it and obey it. Now there is one word of caution that is needed here. We are also to compare Scripture with Scripture. This is a very important matter—remember that the devil can quote Scripture as well, as he did on one occasion with the Lord. But the quotations of the Scriptures by the devil are never balanced. The sword of the Spirit in the devil's hands is an uncouth weapon.

At Sword's Point

Remember how Jesus himself gave us a great example of this when the devil came to tempt him in the wilderness? The devil said to him "If you are the

Son of God, turn these stones into bread." Jesus immediately met him with the sword of the Spirit. He said, "It is written, 'Man shall not live by bread alone [my physical life is not the highest part of my being. I do not have to sustain that, but I do have to sustain my relationship with God. That is the important thing], but by every word that proceeds from the mouth of God'" (Matthew 4:4).

Then the devil tried a new tack. He came to him and said, "Oh well, if you are going to quote Scripture, I can quote it, too. There is a verse in the Psalms, you know, which says that if you get yourself into a dangerous position, God will send his angels to uphold you." Taking him to the top of the temple, the devil said, "If you are the Son of God, throw yourself down; for it is written, 'He will give his angels charge of you . . . lest you strike your foot against a stone'" (Matthew 4:4-5).

But Jesus knew how to handle the devil when he quoted Scripture. He said, "It is written *again* (It is written *again*. I urge you to take note of that. It is not enough to have someone quote a verse of Scripture to you or to have one come flashing into your mind. Compare it. Is it in balance? Is it held in relationship to other truth in the Word of God? "*Again* it is written.), 'You shall not tempt the Lord your God'" (Matthew 4:7). It is that word which delivered him in that hour.

Next, you remember, the devil took him up and showed him all the kingdoms of the world and said, "All these I will give you, if you will fall down and worship me." And again our Lord answered him with the sword of the Spirit. "It is written, 'You shall worship the Lord your God and him only shall you serve'" (Matthew 4:10). Then the account says the devil left him. That is always what happens. He is put to rout by the sword of the Spirit. It is the sword, therefore, that is placed in our hands.

Here then is the Christ's complete armor: you in Christ and Christ in you . . . Christ, demonstrated as truth and experienced as righteousness and peace . . . and Christ, appropriated by faith and applied to life through the hope of salvation and the saying of God. That is all you need. You do not need tranquilizers or expensive psychiatric treatments. You may need some physical therapy now and again, the Word of God has nothing against that, but you will not need all the remedies that science has now made available to give us a chemical bolstering in the hour of anxiety or fear. No, you have the armor of God if you are a Christian.

On the other hand, if you are not a Christian there is no help for you. The place to begin is to become a Christian. The Word of God has no comfort to give those who are not Christians; it has nothing to say to support or encourage someone who is not a Christian. The only way of escape from the allurements and deceitfulness of the enemy is to become a Christian. You must be delivered by the work of Jesus Christ from the kingdom of Satan into the kingdom of God. Then you can put on the armor of God.

Now think it through. Become familiar with this armor. Learn how to use it, and then actually use it when you are under attack. Practice going through this when you feel yourself under attack from Satan. Like a soldier in battle, put it to work. What good is armor if it rusts unused in a closet? No wonder Christians are constantly failing. Though they may have the armor of God, they do not use it.

If you feel yourself growing cold or lukewarm, you are under attack from the wiles of the devil. If you find yourself depressed or discouraged or are bothered with doubts, fears, and anxieties, or if you feel the lure of lusts, the crush of pain, or the numbness of disappointment, what must you do? Systematically, thoughtfully, deliberately, repeatedly, go through these steps we have discussed here. Think through this armor of God.

But do not give up if no immediate change occurs. We are so brainwashed these days into wanting quick results, immediate relief, instant deliverance. Remember, the attack may be prolonged and there are not always quick results. That is why the apostle says, "Having done all, stand." I will say more about that later, but victory is sure if you persevere. Do not give up; it is only a matter of time. For the word of the promise is sure. "Resist the devil and he will flee from you."

> Our Father, what practical import there is in these matters. How helpful this word is in the midst of our pressures, our discouragements, and our tendencies to defeat. Grant to us, Lord, that we will take them seriously and apply this great armor that is given to us in Jesus Christ and thus learn how full and rich and exciting life can be as a Christian, lived in your strength. For we ask in your name, amen.

Pray at all times in the Spirit, with all prayer and supplication. To that end keep alert with all perseverance, making supplication for all the saints, and also for me, that utterance may be given me in opening my mouth boldly to proclaim the mystery of the gospel, for which I am an ambassador in chains; that I may declare it boldly, as I ought to speak (Ephesians 6:18-20).

9
ADVICE WHEN ATTACKED

The apostle Paul has outlined for us three steps we must take if we expect to be strong in the Lord and to resist the attacks of Satan. The first, as we have been discussing, is to put on the armor of God—the *whole* armor—"that you may be able to stand against the wiles of the devil."

And the second step, Paul says, is to pray.

Pray at all times in the Spirit, with all prayer and supplication. To that end keep alert with all perseverance, making supplication for all the saints, and also for me, that utterance may be given me in opening my mouth boldly to proclaim the mystery of

*the gospel, for which I am an ambassador in
chains; that I may declare it boldly, as I ought to
speak (Ephesians 6:18-20).*

There is a very strong and powerful relationship between putting on the armor of God and praying.
These two things belong together; in fact, one grows
out of the other. It is not enough to put on the armor
of God—you must also pray. It is not enough to
pray—you must also have put on the armor of God.

As we have seen, putting on the armor of God is
far from being merely figurative—it is an actual
thing you do. It is remembering what Christ is to you
and thinking through the implications of that relationship in terms of your present struggle and experience. Essentially, putting on the armor is done in
the realm of your thought-life. It is an adjustment of
the attitude of your heart to reality, to things as they
really are. It is thinking through the implications of
the facts revealed in God's Word.

Our problem with life is that we do not see it as it
is; we suffer from strange illusions. This is why we
desperately need and must have the revelation of the
facts of Scripture. Life is what God has declared it to
be. When we face it on that basis, we discover that
revelation is right, it is accurate, it does describe
what is happening. And more, it tells why things
happen and what lies behind them. All this is part of
putting on this armor, of appropriating Christ to life
in terms of your present situation. It is all done in the
realm of the thought-life.

What do you do when you put on the breastplate
of righteousness? You think of Christ and what his
righteousness means as it is imparted to you. What
do you do when you take up the sword of the Spirit?
You give heed, as we saw, to those flashes of Scripture,

those portions of the word of God that come to your mind and have immediate application to the situation you are facing. But again, this is all done in the realm of thought.

At first it takes time to work this all through, but as we learn how to do it, the process becomes much more rapid. We can almost instantaneously think through this line of approach to the problems we are facing. This is what Paul means in the letter to the Corinthians when he says, "take every thought captive to obey Christ" (2 Corinthians 10:5).

Harmful If Not Applied

If we merely think about these things, however, and never bring our thoughts into fulfillment through some form of action, we are actually violating our basic humanity, and this can be dangerous. Human beings are made both to *think* and to *do*—in that order. We receive information first, assimilate it, correlate it, and think it through. And then we act upon what we have both thought and felt. Our emotions and our mind, working upon our will, bring us at last to activity. This is the normal and proper procedure for human living.

All our doing must and will grow out of our thinking. Sometimes we speak of "thoughtless" actions. We say of someone that he acted thoughtlessly. This is impossible. You cannot act thoughtlessly. What we really mean is that someone has acted with very superficial, shallow thinking. But it is actually impossible ever to act without having first thought. Yet it is possible to think without ever acting. That is what the apostle is bringing us to in 2 Corinthians 10:5.

To think without doing is inevitably frustrating. It is like cooking and never eating. You can imagine how frustrating that would be. So the complement to putting on the armor of God and the activity which results from it is to pray. First to think through and then to pray.

Notice that the apostle does not reverse this and instruct us to pray first and then put on the armor of God. That is what we often try to do, and the result is a feeble, impotent prayer life. There is great practical help here if we follow carefully the designated order of Scripture.

I think most Christians, if they were honest, would confess that they were dissatisfied with their prayer life. They feel it is inadequate and perhaps infrequent. All of us at times struggle to improve the quality as well as the quantity of our prayer lives. Sometimes we adopt schedules that we attempt to maintain or we develop long lists of names and projects and places that we try to remember in prayer or we attempt to discipline ourselves in some way to a greater ministry in this realm. In other words, we begin with the doing, but when we do that, we are starting in the wrong place. We are violating our basic human nature in doing it that way. The place to start is not with the doing but with the thinking.

The Place to Start

Now I am not suggesting that there is no place for Christian discipline. There is. I am not suggesting that we won't need to take our wills and put them to a task and follow through. There is this need. But first we should do what is involved in "putting on the armor of God." First think through the implications of our faith, and then prayer will follow naturally and much more easily. It will be thoughtful prayer—that has meaning and relevance.

That is the problem with much of our praying now, is it not? It is so shallow and superficial. What is needed? Prayer should be an outgrowth of thoughtfulness about the implications of faith. That adds depth and significance to it. Prayer should be pointed and purposeful.

Now, basically what is prayer? Is it a mere superstition as some people think, a mumbling, a talking to yourself under the deluded dream that you are addressing deity? Or is it a form of black magic by which some heavenly genie is expected to manipulate life to our desire—a kind of ecclesiastical Aladdin's lamp that we rub? I am afraid many have that concept of prayer. On the other hand, is it, as certain groups tell us, self-communion, a psychological form of talking to yourself in which you discover depths in your being that were there all the time, but you did not realize it until you prayed?

All of these ideas of prayer hold no similarity with what we read in Scripture on the subject. Paul here recognizes two categories of prayer: that which he calls (1) all prayer, and (2) supplication. All prayer is the widest classification; supplication is the specific request that is made in prayer. And if you take the whole range of Bible teaching on this great subject of prayer, you will find that underlying all the biblical presentation of prayer is the idea that it is conversation with God. That is all it is; prayer is simply conversing with God.

Family Talk

As we understand the position of a Christian, a believer, he is in the family of God. Therefore prayer is family talk. It is a friendly, intimate, frank, unrestricted talking with God, and it is into this close and intimate relationship that every individual is brought by faith in Jesus Christ. By faith in Christ we pass out of the realm of being strangers to God and aliens to the family of God into the intimate family circle of the children of God. It is easy to talk within a family circle, but think what harm is done to that intimacy if people refuse to talk within the family circle.

Now supplication is making some specific request. James says, "You do not have, because you do not ask" (James 4:2). In our conversation with God it is perfectly proper to ask, because we are children and he is a Father. What Paul is saying is, "After you have put on the armor of God, after you have thought through the implications of your faith in the ways that have been suggested previously, then talk to God about it." Tell him the whole thing. Tell him your reactions, tell him how you feel, describe your relationship to those around you and your reactions to them, and ask him for what you need.

Prayer is often considered to be such a high and holy thing that it has to be carried on in some artificial language or tone of voice. You hear this frequently from pulpits. Pastors adopt what has been aptly called a "stained-glass voice." They pray as though God were far off in some distant corner of the universe. But prayer is a simple conversation with a Father. It is what the apostle describes beautifully in the Epistle to the Philippians:

> *Have no anxiety about anything, but in everything by prayer and supplication* [there it is again] *with thanksgiving let your requests be made known to God. And the peace of God, which passes all understanding, will keep your hearts and your minds in Christ Jesus (Philippians 4:6-7).*

That is a wonderful study in prayer. Paul is saying there are three simple things involved in prayer. First, worry about nothing: "Be anxious for nothing." Christian friends, do you hear what that says?

Worry about nothing! This is one of the major problems in Christian living today.

Christians are either stumbling blocks to non-Christians or are a glowing testimony and witness to them depending on whether they worry or not. Christians are continually exhorted in Scripture to worry about nothing. Now that doesn't mean not to have a proper interest and concern about things. Stoicism is not advocated here, but we are not to be anxious, fretful, worried.

Nevertheless this is so often the attitude of our lives. Someone said, "I am so loaded up with worries that if anything happened to me this week it would be two weeks before I could get around to worrying about it." Sometimes we make an artificial attempt to cure our worrying by will power. As another has put it,

> *I've joined the new 'Don't worry' Club*
> *And now I hold my breath*
> *I'm so scared I'm going to worry*
> *That I'm worried half to death.*

But the admonition is Worry about nothing, and that is only possible when you have put on the armor of God. Do not try to attempt it on any other basis. Worry comes from fear, and the only thing that will dissolve fear is facts. Therefore to put on the armor of God is to face the facts just as they are.

The second thing Paul says is involved in prayer is to pray about everything. *Everything!* Someone says, do you mean that God is interested in little things as well as big things? Is there anything that is big to God? They are all little things to him. Of course he is interested in them; he says so. The hairs on our head are numbered by him. Jesus was at great pains to show us that God is infinitely involved in the most minute details of our lives. He is concerned about everything. Therefore pray about everything.

And what is the result? "You will be kept through anything!" That is what he says in Philippians. "The peace of God, which passes all understanding." It is a peace which no one can explain, which is there despite the circumstances, and which certainly does not arise out of any change of circumstances. And it "will keep your hearts and your minds in Christ Jesus." Can there be anything more relevant than that in this troubled, anxious, fretful, weary, disturbed world?

An Essential Link

Inherent in prayer are three basic facts. When we pray we recognize first the existence of an invisible kingdom. We would never pray at all if we did not have some awareness that someone is listening, that behind what is visible there is an invisible kingdom. It is not far off in space somewhere; it is right here. It surrounds us on every side. We are constantly in touch with it even though we do not always realize it. It lies behind the facade of life, and all through the Scripture we are exhorted to take heed of this, to reckon with it and deal with it, to acknowledge that it exists.

The second thing that prayer reveals is that we Christians have confidence that the kingdom of God is highly significant, that it affects our lives directly, that the visible things which occur in our world are a direct result of something that is happening in the realm of invisibility. Therefore if you want to change the visibilities, you must start with the invisibilities.

Third, and perhaps the most hotly contested fact by the devil and his forces, is that our prayers play a direct and essential part in bringing God's invisible power to bear on visible life. In other words, God answers prayer. Prayer is purposeful and powerful. It is not pitiful and pathetic pleading with only a rare chance that it might be answered. No, prayer is powerful. God answers! Prayer is an essential link in the working of God in the world today. Without it he often does not work—with it he certainly does. Those three things are all involved in the matter of prayer.

But now we must immediately add that God answers prayer according to his promises. There is a very vague and undefined concept of prayer held by many that God answers any kind of prayer, no matter what you want or how you ask for it. This, of course, results frequently in disappointments and gives rise to the widespread belief that prayer is ineffectual. But God answers every prayer that is based upon a promise.

Prayer does not start with us; it starts with God. God must say he will do something before we are free to ask him to do it. That is the point. That is how it works with a father and his children. No parent commits himself to give his children anything they want or anything they ask for. He makes it clear to them that he will do certain things and not do other things. In the realm of those limits the father commits himself to answer his children's requests. So it is with God. God has given promises, and they form the only proper basis for supplication.

This what is meant here by Paul's reminder that we are to pray at all times in the Spirit. In the Spirit! Here again is a great area of misunderstanding. Many take the phrase "in the Spirit" to be descriptive of the emotions we should have when we pray. They think it is necessary to be greatly moved before prayer can be effectual—that we must always pray with deep earnestness. This is of course possible at times, but it is not essential or necessary to the effectiveness of prayer. And it is certainly not the meaning of this phrase "in the Spirit." It has no relationship to the emotions that we feel in prayer.

If He Promised

Well, what is it then? It means to pray according to the promises which the Spirit has given, and it is based on the character of God which the Spirit has made known. That is praying in the Spirit. God has never promised to answer just any prayer, but he does promise to answer prayer in a way that he has carefully outlined and given to us. He does so invariably and without partiality; he is no respecter of persons in this matter of prayer. In the realm of our personal needs (those needs that call forth most of our prayers) —the need of wisdom, perhaps, or power or patience or grace or strength—God's promise is specifically and definitely to answer immediately. He always answers that type of prayer immediately. "For every one who asks receives" (Luke 11:10).

The apostle is saying in our text that we must take this matter of prayer seriously and learn what God has promised. In other words, master this subject as you would master any other course of study you undertake. Scientists have mastered various areas in the realm of science. Teachers have become proficient at the art of teaching. Artisans give time and study to their trade. In the same way, we must learn to master the art of praying. For though prayer is the simplest thing in the world—a conversation with God—it also can become the very deepest and most profound experience in your life. As you grow in this matter of praying, you will discover that God is very serious about prayer and that through it he makes his omnipotence and omniscience available to us in terms of specific promises.

When you learn to pray on that basis, you will discover that exciting and unexpected things are constantly happening, that there is a quiet but mighty power at work on which you can rely. And as you learn to pray in this way, you find that a tremendous weapon, a mighty power to influence your own life and the lives of others, is put at your disposal.

Open Their Eyes, Lord

But we are not alone in this battle—this conflict with doubt, dismay, fear, confusion, and uncertainty. No, there are others around us who are weaker and younger in Christ than we are, and there are still others who are stronger than we. But all of us are fighting this battle together. We cannot put on the armor of God for another person, but we can pray for that other person. We can call in reinforcements when we find him engaged in a struggle greater than he can handle for the moment, or perhaps for which he is not fully equipped. It may be, you see, that he has not yet learned how to handle his armor adequately. We are to be aware of other people's problems and pray for them. We are to pray that their eyes will be open to danger, and we are to help them realize how much is available in the armor God has given them, for it is a means of specific help and strength for specific trial.

Notice how Paul asks this for himself in this very passage. "[Pray] for me, that utterance may be given me in opening my mouth boldly to proclaim the mystery of the gospel" (Ephesians 6:19). This mighty apostle has a deep sense of his need for prayer. He says, "Pray that God may grant to me boldness that I will be so confident of the truth of which I speak that no fear of man will ever dissuade me or turn me aside." You find another notable example of Paul's desire for prayer in the closing verses of the fifteenth chapter of Romans where he asks the Christians to pray for three things specifically: physical safety when he visits Jerusalem; a sensitive, tactful spirit when he speaks to Christians there; and an ultimate opportunity to visit the city of Rome (Romans 15:30-32). Three specific requests, and the record of Scripture is that every one of them was answered exactly as Paul had asked.

In reading through the prayers of Paul I find that he deals with many matters. He prays repeatedly for other Christians that their spiritual understanding might be enlightened. He asks that the eyes of their mind—their intelligence—might be opened and unveiled. This repetition in the apostle's prayers indicates the importance of intelligently understanding life—what is true and what is false, what is real and what is phony. It also illustrates the power of the devil to blind and confuse us and to make things look very different from the way they really are. So the repeated prayer of the apostle is, Lord, open their eyes that their understanding may be enlightened, that their intelligence may be clarified, that they may see things as they are.

In the letter of James, the importance of praying for others is forcefully underlined. "My brethren, if any one among you wanders from the truth and some one brings him back, let him know that whoever brings back a sinner from the error of his way will save his soul from death and will cover a multitude of sins" (James 5:19, 20).

The prayer of another person can change the whole atmosphere of one person's life, oftentimes overnight. One Christmas eve my family and I were in the Sierra Nevada mountains at Twain Harte. When the sun went down, the landscape around us was dry and barren. A few brown leaves swirled down from the trees; it was a typically bleak winter landscape. But when we awoke the next morning it was to a wonderland of beauty. Every harsh line was softened, every blot was covered. Five inches of snow had fallen during the night and the whole landscape was quietly and marvelously transformed into a fairyland of delight.

I have seen this same thing happen in the life of an individual whose attitude toward the things of God and of reality was hard, stubborn, determined to have his own way. By virtue of prayer, secretly performed in the closet, that person's heart was softened, melted, mellowed, and changed. His total outlook was changed overnight.

Now it does not always happen overnight. Sometimes it takes much longer. Time is a factor which God alone controls, and he never puts a time limit on his instruction concerning prayers. But he constantly calls us to this ministry of prayer both for ourselves and for one another. When we learn to pray as God teaches us to pray, we release in our own lives and in the lives of others the immense resources of God to strengthen the spirit and to give inner stability and power to meet the pressures and problems of life.

> *Our Father, we know so little about this mighty ministry of prayer. We pray that you will teach us to pray. Forgive us for the way we have often looked at prayer as though it were unimportant, insignificant, an optional thing in our lives. Help us to take it seriously. Help us to realize that you have made this the point of contact between us and you. We pray, then, as the disciples prayed, "Lord teach us to pray." In thy name, amen.*

10
THE INFALLIBLE POSTURE

Our study has led us now to the third and last admonition of Paul, which is the aim and thrust of this entire passage. It is given to us in only one word, but a word which is repeated four different times in these verses. It is the word *stand*. Notice how it punctuates these phrases:

> *Put on the whole armor of God, that you may be able to* stand *against the wiles of the devil. . . . Therefore take the whole armor of God, that you may be able to* withstand *in the evil day, and having done all, to* stand. Stand *therefore . . . (Ephesians 6:11, 13, 14).*

Everything aims at our ability to stand. What does it mean? I have often been impressed in watching a football game to see the defending team's response to an especially hard push by their opponents. If they have an advantage in score, the defenders will sometimes simply line up on the scrimmage line against the rush of the opposing team and refuse to budge. That is exactly what this word pictures to us. We are to refuse to move from the ground of faith we have taken, refuse to yield ground. Having done all (and only then), we are to stand.

Now why did the apostle put it this way? Why doesn't he say, having done all, fight? Why does he not use some military term that speaks of moving out —advance or charge? We must take these words seriously, for after all, these are not just words that might be used in a children's game. They are commands given in a very serious fight. The apostle uses the word *stand* because it is the only proper word to use. It is the only word which describes the final attitude we must have to insure absolute victory.

As we look at this word more carefully, we can see that it touches on three aspects of the struggle of life. First, the use of this word *stand* reveals to us the intensity of the struggle in which we are involved. We are told to stand because there are times when that is all we can do. The most we can possibly hope to achieve at times is simply to stand unmoved. There are times in battle when a soldier can do no more than try to protect himself and stay where he is. The intensity of the conflict becomes so furious, so fierce, there is nothing else he can do but simply hold his ground. That is what this word implies to us.

Paul has already spoken in this passage about evil days which come. Thank God, all of life does not consist of evil days, but evil days do come. These are days when circumstances simply stagger us, when we face some combination of events—some disheartening tragedy or circumstance—that almost knocks us off our feet, and we can do nothing else but hope to stand where we are.

There are times when doubts plague us. We are exposed to intellectual attacks, and we have all we can do to assert any degree of faith at all. We find ourselves in situations and circumstances when we are overwhelmed with fears and anxieties and can scarcely keep our heads because of the pressure. There are times when indifference seems to sap our spiritual strength so much that we lose all our vitality. It drains away our will to act, and we seem unable to make ourselves do the simplest things to maintain faith.

This is all part of the struggle. We get disturbed when there seems to be no growth in our Christian faith. Our ministry or our witness appears to be impossible or ineffective. All the challenge and keenness of our spiritual life is gone. What are we to do then? Paul says we are to gird up our loins, put on the whole armor of God, pray—and having done all, stand! Putting on the armor and praying will not necessarily change the circumstance. Then what? Then stand! Stay right where you are. Refuse to move, refuse to think any more. Stand right where you are until the attack lessens. This is the final word.

Cycles of Trouble.

Everywhere the Word of God warns us that as we draw nearer to the time of our Lord's return, evil days will come more frequently. The Bible has always told us that there will be evil days, but sometimes we read certain predictions wrongly. There is a passage in Timothy, for instance, that refers to the latter times.

"Now the Spirit expressly says that in latter times some will depart from the faith by giving heed to deceitful spirits and doctrines of demons" (1 Timothy 4:1). We read that as though it were a prediction of the closing moments of the age. But "latter times" means the whole of the age from our Lord's first coming until his second. Paul is not talking about one particular time of trouble reserved for the last moment; he is talking about repetitive cycles of trouble that come again and again throughout the whole course of these latter days.

But the Word also suggests that these cycles become fiercer in intensity and more widespread in their impact as the age draws to its close. There is a growing awareness in our day that we live in a one-world community. We are no longer separated from other peoples by great distances of thought or time. What happens on the other side of the world today affects us tomorrow. We are very much aware of this. Evil days were once limited geographically. In the past, persecution grew intense in various places, and economic pressures became severe in certain areas, while in other parts of the world things were fine. But now, as the age goes on, these areas of trouble become more widespread. Now they are worldwide in their impact.

Surely we do not have to press this point. In America we must realize we are living in an island of relative peace and security in the midst of an enormous sea of trouble and distress. That sea is constantly eroding away our relative security. It is an irresistible, rising tide, the lappings of whose waters we can already hear. Conditions are not getting better in our world; they are worsening. Any honest person, facing world conditions, must admit this. The vaunted solutions of sincere men, such as education, scientific discoveries, economic improvements, better legislation, are not working. Of course such solutions have their place, and I am not suggesting that they be discarded. But they are not solving the problem. It is getting worse, for as we have seen all along, the issue never lies in these superficial, surface things. It lies much deeper in the hearts and souls of men under the control of a cruel and irresistible power that dominates the world, which Paul refers to as "the world rulers of this present darkness." Only the delivering strength of Jesus Christ is adequate to deal with them. This is being confirmed to us from rather unexpected sources these days. Listen to these words from a contemporary non-Christian writer.

> *I remind you of what is happening in the great cities of the earth today: Chicago, Detroit, Pittsburgh, London, Manchester, Paris, Tokyo, Hong Kong and the rest. These cities are for the most part vast pools of human misery, networks of raw human nerves exposed without benefit of illusion or hope to the new godless world wrought by industrial man. The people in these cities are lost. Some of them are so lost that they no longer even know it, and they are the real lost ones. They haunt the movies for distraction. They gamble. They depress their sensibilities with alcohol, or they seek strong sensations to dull their sense of a meaningless existence (Richard Wright,* The Outsider).

That is the world we are facing now, and because of it there are many who are faltering in their faith. All too often we read in the newspapers of outstanding Christian leaders who have suffered moral collapse and have been laid on the shelf, their ministry and their testimony brought to an end. This is happening everywhere.

To Reveal the False

Now, God is permitting this in order to separate the phony from the true. He says he will do this; the Word makes it very clear. There is a passage in Hebrews in which we are told definitely that the things which can be shaken will be shaken. God is allowing these testings to reveal the genuine and to remove what can be shaken in order that what cannot be shaken might remain (Hebrews 12:26-27). Therefore evil days come. When they come into your own personal experience, you will need to remember that the Word of God to you is to put on the whole armor of God, to pray, and then stand. Perhaps you will realize that there is nothing else you can do, but you can win if you will stand.

Not long ago I ran across a letter from a missionary out in the jungles of New Guinea writing to his friends at home. He has caught the very spirit of our Christian faith in these words:

> *Man, it is great to be in the thick of the fight, to draw the old devil's heaviest guns, to have him at you with depression and discouragement, slander, disease. He doesn't waste time on a lukewarm bunch. He hits good and hard when a fellow is hitting him. You can always measure the weight of your blow by the one you get back. When you're on your back with fever and at your last ounce of strength, when some of your converts backslide, when you learn that your most promising inquirers are only fooling, when your mail gets held up, and some don't bother to answer your letters, is that the time to put on mourning? No, sir. That's the time to pull out the stops and shout, Hallelujah! The old fellow's getting it in the neck and hitting back. Heaven is leaning over the battlements and watch-*

ing. "Will he stick it?" And as they see Who is
with us, as they see the unlimited reserves, the
boundless resources, as they see the impossibility of
failure, how disgusted and sad they must be when
we run away. Glory to God! We're not going to
run away. We're going to stand.

Now there is a second thing indicated by this word
stand. It indicates to us the character of the battle the
Christian faces. The act of standing implies a defensive action primarily. The proper defense will win the
day. I know that is often misunderstood, for we frequently hear the saying, "The best defense is a good
offense." But if a castle is under attack from an army,
the battle is not won by those in the castle venturing
forth to overwhelm the army outside. The battle is
won by repelling all invasion. This is a picture of our
Christian life. This is a defensive battle. We are not
out to take new ground; we are to defend that which
is already ours.

In the Christian battle the offensive work was done
nearly two thousand years ago at the cross and the resurrection. The Lord Jesus is the only one who has the
power and strength to take the offense in this great
battle with the prince of darkness. But he has done
that. All that we possess as believers is already given
to us. We do not fight for it. We do not battle to be
saved or fight to be justified or forgiven or accepted
into the family of God. All these things are given to
us. They were won by Another who, in the words of
Paul in Colossians, "disarmed the principalities and
powers and made a public example of them, triumph-
ing over them in him" (Colossians 2:15).

No New Ground

But we are to fight to use all this, to enjoy it, to
fully experience it. The enemy is trying to keep us

from realizing what we have and from using it to the full. There is where the battle lines are. We do not need to take new ground as Christians. We cannot do this. All of that has been accomplished and given to us. As Jude says, in almost the last word of the New Testament, "contend for the faith which was once for all delivered to the saints" (Jude 3). We are to hold on to that which God gives us and not let any of it be lost or taken from us. That is what "contend for the faith" means. It does not mean to attack everyone who does not agree with you. It means to hold on to what God has already given you and utilize it to the full. As Paul writes to the Corinthians, "stand firm in your faith, be courageous, be strong" (1 Corinthians 16:13). Do not surrender an inch of ground even though others do.

Well, someone says, this is so negative, so defensive. I don't like to hear such talk. It sounds as though Christians are to cover their heads and avoid all contact with the world while trying somehow to get through life and on to heaven without becoming contaminated. That, of course, is exactly the interpretation which the devil wants us to have of this word *stand*. It is defensive action, but the amazing thing is that this kind of defensive action becomes the greatest offense the Christian can mount.

The fact is, the Christian who learns to stand, to give up no segment of his faith but to put on the armor of God and to pray and thus be unmovable, is the only one who in any way will or can touch the world around him. He is the only one who will reflect the love of Christ in the midst of unlovely situations. He is the only one who will be able to manifest peace and certainty and poise and assurance in the midst of a very troubled and unhappy world.

Christians who learn to stand make possible some

degree of rest and enjoyment for the world. We are the salt of the earth, Jesus said. Ah, but if the salt has lost its savor, what good is it? It is good for nothing but to be cast out and trodden under the feet of men! That is by and large what the world is doing with the church these days—treading it under foot as worthless, useless. That is because we have not learned to stand.

But when a Christian learns this, it is the very fact that he can stand when everyone else is falling that draws the attention of others and makes them seek his secret. People will stop, look, listen, and say, "What is it that these people have? They don't give way like we do; they don't go along with the rest of the crowd. They seem to be able to resist these compelling pressures that we so easily give in to."

That is what manhood is. That is what God is after. That is what he wants to make us in Christ. But the purpose of the battle is not to *become* that kind of a man, for that is precisely the kind of man Christ makes us when we follow him. The battle is to show it, to reveal it, to manifest what we are, and thus to refuse to believe the lies that keep us weak and make us act like an animal rather than a man. Put on the whole armor of God—all that Christ is—pray, and having done all, stand!

Now, there is a third thing suggested by the word *stand,* and that is the certainty of victory. If putting on the armor of God and prayer make it possible to stand unmoved and unmovable, then there is nothing more required to win. After all, if a castle cannot be taken, the attacking army has nothing left to do but to withdraw. There is nothing else they can do. They are defeated, beaten.

I have discussed at considerable length the cleverness of Satan, his subtlety of attack—"the wiles of the devil"—and the impossibility of defeating him by human wisdom. Every saint in the record of Scripture, every believer throughout history, has been at one time or another defeated by the devil when he tried to match wits with the devil in his own strength. This is true. But it is also true that when any saint, any believer—even the newest and the weakest—stands in the strength of Christ, puts on the whole armor of God, and in dependence upon the presence of God in prayer, stands, the devil is always defeated.

The Fatal Flaw

This is because of a basic weakness, a fatal flaw in the devil's approach. When the believer stands on the ground of faith, the devil always overreaches himself. He goes too far. He commits himself to extremes, and in that lies his defeat. Sooner or later the reality which is truth must become apparent. The devil can never take the ground of truth because that, of course, would defeat his own aims. He cannot defend and support God, for he is out to attack and outwit him. Because God is truth, all that the devil can do is take the ground of untruth, of extremes, distortions, wrongness. Ultimately, because God is truth (and truth is always the reflection of God) and God never changes, truth must finally prevail. That has been true throughout the entire history of the world, and it will be the continuing record from now on.

Abraham Lincoln expressed it well in that famous quotation, "It is possible to fool some of the people all of the time, and all of the people some of the time, but it is impossible to fool all of the people all of the time." Truth comes out. God is truth. If we live with it long enough, stand on it long enough, it will prevail and reveal itself.

This explains what we have referred to at times as "the phenomenon of fashions in evil." Anyone who has been a Christian for a considerable period of time learns that error comes in cycles, like clothing styles. You may be out of style for awhile, but if you stay with the same one long enough it will come back in. If you are standing on the truth of God, there will be times when it is regarded with utter scorn by the world. The truth will be laughed at and you will be mocked. But if you follow those foolish people who think they must adjust to every sweeping current of the times and try to maintain what they call "intellectual respectability" at all times, you will find that as fast as you adjust, styles change and you are out of style again.

But if you continue to stand fast on what God has declared unchangeable, you will find a strange phenomenon happening: The very truths that ten years ago were looked down upon and laughed at and scorned by the world will come into fashion again and be held up as the newest discovery of the brilliant intellect of men. Then you who have believed it right along are right back in style again. Truth never changes.

The devil must ultimately be defeated if you will simply stand on what God has said. We might even feel a little sorry for the devil, for it is his cruel fate to be continually defeated by the very weapons which he tries to use against God and his people. That is why it is so foolish to believe the lies of the devil.

I often think the devil is like the villain in the old Western melodramas. Remember how the plot always develops? The heroine appears to be doomed, and the villain always appears to have the upper hand as he twirls his mustache and rubs his hands together. But at the critical moment the hero arrives and the

plot changes. The villain is beaten by his own devices, and he slinks off the stage muttering, "Curses!
Foiled again!" Now, that is the devil's fate when he
attacks any Christian who is willing to stand.

The cross is the great example of this. The cross
looked like the supreme achievement of the devil, the
supreme moment of victory when all the powers of
darkness were howling with glee as they saw the Son
of God beaten and wounded, rejected and despised,
hanging upon a cross, naked, before all the world. It
looked like the triumph of darkness. Jesus said it
was. "This is your hour," he said, "and the power of
darkness."

But it was at that very moment the devil lost. In
the cross all that he had risked was defeated, beaten
down, and the devil and all his angels were disarmed
and openly displayed as defeated by the power of
Jesus Christ. This is what God does all through life.
The devil sends sickness, defeat, death, darkness,
pain, suffering, and tragedy. It is all the work of
Satan. But that is not the whole of the story. God
takes those very things and uses them to strengthen
us and bless us, to teach us and enlarge us and fulfill
us—if we stand. This is the whole of the story.

The Final Issue

Here is a statement from a Christian man who has
been an invalid all his life. He is one of those lonely,
obscure people who live in constant pain, who does
not know what it means to be able to use his physical
body in any way except in pain and suffering. But he
writes this:

> *Loneliness is not a thing of itself, not an evil sent to
> rob us of the joys of life. Loneliness, loss, pain, sor-
> row, these are disciplines, God's gifts to drive us to*

his very heart, to increase our capacity for him, to sharpen our sensitivities and understanding, to temper our spiritual lives so that they may become channels of his mercy to others and so bear fruit for his kingdom. But these disciplines must be seized upon and used, not thwarted. It must not be seen as excuses for living in the shadow of half-lives, but as messengers, however painful, to bring our souls into vital contact with the Living God, that our lives may be filled to overflowing with himself in ways that may, perhaps, be impossible to those who know less of life's darkness.

Now that is what it means to stand. One of these days, the Bible says, the struggle will end. It will end for all of us at the end of our lives, but it may end before that in the coming of the Lord. Some day it will be over; there is no doubt of that. And some day it will be written of some, as it is recorded in the book of Revelation, "They have conquered him [the great dragon, the devil] by the blood of the Lamb and by the word of their testimony for they loved not their lives even unto death" (Revelation 12:11). The great issue of life is not how much money we make or how much favor we gather or how much of a name we make for ourselves. The great issue, above all, is whether it can be written of us as we come to the end that we overcame by the blood of the Lamb and by the word of our testimony, for we loved not our lives unto death.

These are perilous days, our Father. But we thank you, Lord, that we do not get our view of life from the newspapers, but from the reality of your living Word. Help us to believe it and obey it and thus to stand, undefeated and undefeatable. In Christ's name, amen.